"This important practical guide to policymaking in UK higher education brings together the perspectives of a range of actors and commentators on how the policy process has been transformed in the last few years. Bagshaw and McVitty are to be commended for plugging a gap in the literature, between policy comment and academic analysis. They, and their contributors, intelligently explore the messy, complex and contingent nature of policymaking and the politics that surround it, in engaging and refreshing ways. If you're interested in actually shaping policy and influencing the politics surrounding higher education – in the UK or elsewhere – this book is for you."

Professor William Locke, Director
Melbourne Centre for the Study of Higher Education
University of Melbourne
Australia

Influencing Higher Education Policy

Drawing together a team of expert contributors from across the sector to offer contemporary descriptions and critical reflection of practice in higher education, *Influencing Higher Education Policy* uncovers the nature of policymaking and interpretation. With a suite of authors whose experiences range from governmental to academic, this book shares insights from professionals working in the field of higher education policy to provide useful, practical, and implementable information.

Placing focus on professional aspects, and with practical examples bringing to light experiences, insights, and recommendations across policy and public affairs, this book is divided into three parts. It covers concepts and theories for policy influence, regulation and the role of government, and institutions' engagement with policy. Furthermore, it considers:

- what it means to work in policy and public affairs in higher education;
- the increased complexity and fluidity of higher education politics;
- regulatory reforms in higher education;
- the position of the student in policy discourses.

Offering a contemporary representation, *Influencing Higher Education Policy* is an indispensable guide for all those who work in higher education, particularly those who work in communications, strategy, planning, and leadership roles.

Ant Bagshaw is a management consultant at Nous Group, working across its Australian and UK education practices. Prior to joining Nous he was Deputy CEO at Wonkhe. He has also worked as a policy and projects officer for senior management teams at the London School of Economics and University of Kent, and in a policy development role at University College London.

Debbie McVitty is Editor of Wonkhe. She is a former chief of staff at Universities UK, policy director at the University of Bedfordshire and the National Union of Students, and a founding member of Wonkhe's editorial group.

Influencing Higher Education Policy

A Professional Guide to Making an Impact

Edited by Ant Bagshaw and Debbie McVitty

Routledge
Taylor & Francis Group

LONDON AND NEW YORK

First published 2020
by Routledge
2 Park Square, Milton Park, Abingdon, Oxon, OX14 4RN

and by Routledge
52 Vanderbilt Avenue, New York, NY 10017

Routledge is an imprint of the Taylor & Francis Group, an informa business

British Library Cataloguing-in-Publication Data
A catalogue record for this book is available from the British Library

Library of Congress Cataloging-in-Publication Data
Names: Bagshaw, Ant, editor. | McVitty, Debbie, editor.
Title: Influencing higher education policy: a professional guide to making an impact/Edited by Ant Bagshaw and Debbie McVitty.
Identifiers: LCCN 2019017808 | ISBN 9781138347052 (hardback) | ISBN 9781138347076 (paperback) | ISBN 9780429437120 (ebook)
Subjects: LCSH: Higher education and state. | Education, Higher–Aims and objectives. | Educational change.
Classification: LCC LC171 .I44 2020 | DDC 379–dc23
LC record available at https://lccn.loc.gov/2019017808

ISBN: 978-1-138-34705-2 (hbk)
ISBN: 978-1-138-34707-6 (pbk)
ISBN: 978-0-429-43712-0 (ebk)

Typeset in Minion
by Deanta Global Publishing Services, Chennai, India

Contents

Contributor biographies

Ant Bagshaw is a management consultant at Nous Group, working across its Australian and UK education practices. Prior to joining Nous in October 2018, he was Deputy CEO at Wonkhe. He has also worked as a policy and projects officer for senior management teams at the London School of Economics and University of Kent, and in a policy development role at University College London; he was an institutional reviewer for the Quality Assurance Agency for Higher Education for six years, and he started his career working on student engagement policy at the National Union of Students. A graduate of the University of Cambridge, Cardiff University, and The Open University, he is studying for an education doctorate at the University of Sheffield. Ant is also a member of the council of The Dyson Institute of Engineering and Technology.

Diana Beech is Policy Adviser to the Minister of State for Universities, Science, Research and Innovation. She was appointed by Sam Gyimah MP in August 2018. Prior to this, Diana was the first Director of Policy and Advocacy at the Higher Education Policy Institute. Diana holds a PhD in German Studies from the University of Cambridge and has held academic positions at universities in Canada, Germany, and the UK.

Selena Bolingbroke is the Lead for External Engagement and Strategic Development at Goldsmiths. She wrote the first Community Engagement

Strategy and now directs the development of the university's civic partnerships. Selena has worked across HE, local, and central government in a range of roles which share a focus on skills-led regeneration, strategic development, and community engagement. Past roles include Pro Vice-Chancellor at University of East London, Director of Local Strategic Partnership for Thurrock, and Skills Lead for Thames Gateway Strategic Executive in the Office of the Deputy Prime Minister.

Anna Bradshaw began working in HE as a students' union sabbatical officer at the University of Oxford, where she represented women. She has since worked in HE policy at Universities Scotland, the British Council (Scotland) and Advance HE (formerly the Equality Challenge Unit). She currently works as a Senior Policy Adviser in the public policy team at The British Academy, where she leads the Academy's programme of work on cohesive societies. She combines this professional experience with a keen academic interest in understanding policymaking, and will complete a part-time MSc in Social Policy (Research) from the London School of Economics in 2019.

Sean Byrne specialises in organisational strategy for public services, and has a background in the British civil service and management consultancy. He helps businesses and government departments develop their response to changes in their external environment and has helped launch new services in a range of sectors including infrastructure, local government, and HE.

Josie Cluer is a Partner and leads the education transformation practice at EY. She is a former special adviser to the Secretary of State for Innovation, Universities and Skills. She writes here in a personal capacity.

Megan Dunn began working in HE as President of Aberdeen University Students' Association. She went on to hold the position of NUS Vice-President (Higher Education), then NUS National President, where she contributed to key policy debates across the sector. She has worked in HE policy at Advance HE (formerly the Equality Challenge Unit) and has chaired the Student Interest Advisory Panel at the Office for Students. She currently works as a senior policy officer in the skills policy team at the Greater London Authority, where she leads on apprenticeship policy. Megan has taken on a number of board positions throughout her career, including with the Higher Education Funding Council for England and the Office of the Independent Adjudicator for Higher Education, and is currently a school governor.

Colette Fletcher has been the Assistant Vice-Chancellor at the University of Winchester since September 2015. Prior to joining the university she was the Head of Policy at Bournemouth University, and has previously held roles at the Higher Education Funding Council for England and the Quality Assurance Agency for Higher Education. After receiving a BSc in Biological Sciences from the University of Birmingham in 2001, Colette went on to study for an MSc in Palaeobiology at the University of Bristol. She is currently studying for a doctorate in Business Administration in Higher Education Management at the University of Bath, specialising in student satisfaction and experience. Colette is the Chair of the Board of the National Network for the Education of Care Leavers, a Governor of Barton Peveril College, a Trustee of the British Accreditation Council, a Trustee of the 401 Foundation (a charity devoted to building confidence and self-esteem and tackling mental health and self-development issues), a Member of the Institute of Risk Managers, a Member of the UK Speechwriters' Guild, and a Fellow of the Royal Society of Arts.

Chris Hale is Director of Policy at Universities UK. He is responsible for the development and management of UUK's policy work, produced largely by an in-house team of programme managers, economists, and analysts. Before being appointed Director in 2015, Chris was Assistant Director of Policy at UUK and led on a number of areas of work, including efficiency and effectiveness and the regulation of HE. Chris has significant expertise in research policy, working as a policy adviser on this issue for UUK for a number of years. Prior to working at UUK, Chris worked at the General Medical Council, and he holds a degree from the University of Sussex and MSc in Public Policy from University College London. He is also the vice-chair of a primary school federation in South East London.

William Hammonds is a policy manager and researcher interested in the policy of HE, culture, race, integration, and terrorism and extremism. William leads UUK's work on regulation, including the passage and implementation of the Higher Education and Research Act 2017, the set-up of the Office for Students and the development of the Teaching Excellence and Student Outcomes Framework. Prior to joining UUK, William worked in politics, local government, and consultancy, working with UK and European organisations such as the European Commission and Arts Council England. He has studied at the University of Exeter, London School of Economics and has a PhD in Government from the University of Essex. His PhD examined the development of the Prevent counter-terrorism policy between 2001 and 2011.

Dewi Knight is Specialist Adviser for Education Reform, Welsh Government. Dewi returned to Wales in 2016 to advise Kirsty Williams and other ministers in driving forward the largest education reform programme anywhere in the UK in the last 50 years. Before that, he worked on UK–China education policy and relations for the British Council, helping to secure international agreements on transnational quality assurance, student mobility, and government co-operation. Prior to that, he was Director of Policy and Adviser to the Vice-Chancellor at the University of Bedfordshire, having previously led on policy and public affairs for The Open University in Wales. He is an International Politics and International History graduate of Aberystwyth University.

Iain Mansfield is a former senior civil servant. He was the principal official at the Department for Education responsible for the design of the Teaching Excellence and Student Outcomes Framework and also worked extensively on a range of other topics in HE, including the Higher Education and Research Act (2017), quality assurance, and student choice. He was part of the team that carried out the 2013 Triennial Review of the Research Councils and, in an early career role, served as Private Secretary to the Director General for Science and Innovation. He joined the Council at Bath Spa University in August 2018. In 2014 he was the winner of the Institute for Economic Affairs' Brexit prize, awarded for the best policy blueprint for the UK should it leave the EU, and is also the author of the fantasy novel *Imperial Visions* and quiz book *The Twelve Quizzes of Christmas*.

Debbie McVitty is Editor of Wonkhe, with responsibility for Wonkhe's daily insight, debate and analysis of HE policy. She was formerly Chief of Staff at Universities UK, Director of Policy at the University of Bedfordshire, and Head of Policy at the National Union of Students. She holds a DPhil in English Literature from the University of Oxford and a Master's in research in HE Policy, Evaluation and Enhancement from Lancaster University.

Cathy Mitchell is an assistant director in the Access, Skills and Outcome Agreement Directorate of the Scottish Funding Council. Having previously led the Performance Measurement and Analysis team at SFC, Cathy has worked across the qualitative and quantitative sides of institutional performance measurement and management of the Scottish university and college sectors. Cathy has an MSc in Social Research with a focus on HE, and also holds an LLB in Law and an MSc in Criminology and Criminal Justice, all from the University of Edinburgh.

Rille Raaper is Assistant Professor in the School of Education, Durham University where her research interests lie in the sociology of HE. She is particularly interested in the neoliberalisation of university policies and practices, the consumerist positioning of students, and student politics. She has conducted numerous research projects on consumer discourse in HE and its impact on students as learners and citizens as well as political agents.

Claire Randerson is Principal Lecturer in the School of Social and Political Sciences at the University of Lincoln. Claire studied History and Politics at the University of Lancaster and International Studies at the University of Birmingham before taking up a lecturing position on the International Relations degree at the University of Lincoln. She teaches and researches in the fields of international relations, internationalisation of HE and genocide studies.

Jessica Strenk joined Middlesex University London as Policy and Public Affairs Manager in 2017. Establishing a new policy and public affairs function at Middlesex, Jessica works closely with the Vice-Chancellor, executive and communications teams providing strategic advice, briefing, policy analysis, leading consultation responses, political engagement, and thought leadership activity. Before joining Middlesex, Jessica worked in public affairs for the infrastructure company Balfour Beatty and as European Policy Manager at Universities UK. Jessica also worked in the European Commission and was Parliamentary Advisor to Nick Clegg in the European Parliament in Brussels 2000–2004. Jessica graduated with a First-Class Honours in Modern Languages from the University of Manchester and has a Master's in Language, Society and Change in Europe from Queen Mary University of London.

Tess Winther is a former student (undergraduate and postgraduate) and staff member at Goldsmiths, and gained her initial experiences working with the student voice and civic engagement at the university. Her work continues to centre on the enhancement of students' voices within universities, especially student representation in institutional governance structures. Additionally, Tess's focus on civic engagement is around how universities can calibrate aspects of their student engagement to enable students to participate in civic culture through their university and contribute in ways that create shared experiences and skills development.

Adam Wright is Deputy Head of Policy (Higher Education and Skills) at The British Academy. He spent several years working in education policy at the National Union of Students and The Royal Society, and previously taught political theory at the University of Essex, where he currently acts as an external member of University Council. His research focuses on poststructuralist and post-Marxist theories of education, and policy enactment and refraction in educational settings.

Acknowledgements

The editors are indebted to the authors, without whom the project simply could not have happened. The authors have contributed their knowledge, shared their experience, and expressed their ideas above and beyond what had been expected of them.

Wonkhe has been an incredible force for opening up the policy debates in higher education. Its founder, Mark Leach, has been an inspiration to many and the success of the organisation he founded – through its reach and influence – is down to his dedication and vision for improving higher education through analysis, debate, and humour. Wonkhe's success has come from its many hundreds of contributors who also deserve recognition for their commitment to shining lights in every obscure area of the higher education sector's many policy debates. And, of course, to the team at Wonkhe for working with diligence and energy to make it all happen. The editors are indebted to Mark – as a colleague, friend and policy wonk – for his support for this book.

Thanks are also due to Sarah Tuckwell and Lisa Font at Routledge for their work bringing this project to fruition. And to the following people for providing inspiration, advice, and encouragement along the way: Richard Brabner, Laura Burley, Helen Carasso, Annie Jackson, Tom Kennie, William Locke, Suzi Macpherson, Robin Middlehurst, Alex Miles, Lizzy O'Shea, Liz Shutt, Lucinda Parr, Gareth Parry, Jacqueline Stevenson, Jen Summerton, Greg Walker, Graeme Wise, and Jonathan Woodhead.

For HRAB and MML

Introduction
Ant Bagshaw and Debbie McVitty

The genesis for this book was a realisation that while there has been a proliferation of roles within universities focusing on policy and public affairs – positions which both editors have held – there is relatively little literature to support the development of this profession within higher education (HE). There is a great deal published about HE policy, be that on Wonkhe – the home of HE policy, at which both editors have also worked – or through the longer-established trade press, from think-tanks or in academic journals and research publications. But there is a gap for bringing together the voices and perspectives of those working across policy and public affairs – the emergent HE "policy wonk" (Leach 2012) – to share experiences, insights, and recommendations.

Here we have assembled a broad slate of authors, from those with experience in universities in different parts of the UK, and in a cross-section of the sector, to those with experience of government (civil service and political advisers) and academics working on HE policy issues. The book is very deliberately *a professional guide*: there is engagement with the academic literature, but the primary emphasis is on sharing the experience of professionals working in this field with a desire to provide interesting and practical information from which others can draw ideas to use in their own contexts.

The geographic emphasis of the work is the UK, and with a further focus on England, and while there are general lessons for influencing policy, the temporal context is largely the reforms and policy agendas for the 2010s. Many of the chapters pick up on the changes to the HE sector resulting from the decision in 2012 to increase undergraduate tuition fees in England and the regulatory reforms in the Higher Education and Research Act 2017. We have not restricted the work to England, and have chapters covering important developments in Wales and Scotland, as well as a reflection on the transnational impact of the Organisation for Economic Cooperation and Development (OECD) on the UK context. We believe that the core skills of understanding policymaking – and identifying ways in which individuals, institutions or groups can influence the policy process – are applicable more widely, to other sectors and in other local, regional, national, or international contexts. Ultimately, this will be part of an evolving literature, as those working in policy and public affairs within universities, sector agencies, and associated organisations – the policy influencers and wonks – develop their profession. We present the content of the book to challenge, to spark ideas and discussion, and to support colleagues in collective pursuit of an HE sector which is healthy, sustainable, and able to achieve the many positive outcomes – in education, research, and many other areas – which those working in HE seek to achieve.

The book is divided into three sections; as a collection of individual essays it is not intended to be read in a linear way, but we have grouped the chapters into three parts:

1. Concepts and theories for policy influence
2. Regulation and the role of government
3. Institutions' engagement with policy

In Part 1, "Concepts and theories for policy influence", we begin with an exploration of "political controversies". Debbie McVitty explores the background to the current state of HE policymaking in Chapter 1, "Power and influence in higher education policymaking: who controls the debate?" She explores the key political debates which provide the context for HE policy and identifies recent trends including government and regulator hostility, the voices of students and academics, and the power of an inclusive policymaking environment. Chapter 2, "Preparing for politics with a capital P", is by Josie Cluer and Sean Byrne, who were both special advisers working in government: they have witnessed at first hand the way in which some topics rise to the very top of the political agenda. This provides a useful context in which to think about the nature of policy and politics. It also identifies a theme – which can be read across other chapters – of the irrationality in policymaking. Anna Bradshaw and Megan Dunn in Chapter 3, "Evidence and policy: theoretical approaches for higher education policymaking", pick this up as they apply models for policy production to the HE sector. Bradshaw and Dunn began their careers in student politics and they now work in policy roles. They make the case for applying theory when interrogating the policymaking process.

The following three chapters in Part 1 consider the role of different organisations and groups in influencing policy. In Chapter 4, "Working with thinktanks", Diana Beech considers the role of these third-party organisations and the influence that they have on the policymaking process. As a former Director of Policy and Advocacy at the Higher Education Policy Institute, Beech is able to draw on her experience working within an HE-focused think-tank to explain the work they do, and how they influence policy. As an example of an international policy organisation, the OECD is a useful demonstration of a non-UK-focused body with a strong interest in HE. Claire Randerson in Chapter 5, "International organisations in higher education policymaking: the role of the OECD", looks at the body's outputs, data and areas of influence to lift up the interrogation of the domestic context to add a supranational dimension. The first part concludes with Chapter 6, "Contesting student identities: making sense of students' positioning in higher education policy", from Adam Wright and Rille Raaper. This chapter searches for the position of the student within the HE policy discourses and considers them as both subjects of, and actors in, HE policymaking.

In Part 2, "Regulation and the role of government", we begin with a consideration of how government in Westminster and Whitehall is able to effect change in HE. This is first considered in Chapter 7, "Higher education policymaking from the government's perspective", in which former civil servant Iain Mansfield considers the different ways in which government can use policy levers to effect change in the HE sector. In Chapter 8, "Lessons from the legislative process: how representative groups shape government policy and legislation", the lens shifts to that of the representative body's role in influencing legislative change, one of the key tools of government policymaking. William Hammonds and Chris Hale, who both work in Universities UK's policy team, explain how the organisation engaged throughout the evolution of the Higher Education and Research Act 2017. They consider the trade-offs between being a critical friend of government and an opponent to reform.

Part 2 also contains two case studies reflecting the experience of two of the UK's devolved administrations. In Chapter 9, "Delivering Diamond: a policy development case study of student funding in Wales", Dewi Knight recounts the development of a major new policy initiative in Wales from the point of view of a specialist policy adviser. Chapter 10, "Performance measurement and student information in the UK: adapting to a diverging policy context between Scotland and England", by Cathy Mitchell from the Scottish Funding Council, presents another example of the divergent approaches across UK HE. In both cases, we see the spillover effects of English policy development and the contrasting ideological approaches to the regulation of HE.

The final section, Part 3, "Institutions' engagement with policy", looks from the position of universities and their staff in the HE policymaking process. Colette Fletcher, in Chapter 11, "A study in imperfection: five lessons on how to influence with impact", shares lessons she has learned from working at Bournemouth University and the University of Winchester, as well as time in sector agencies. Jessica Strenk, who has pioneered the establishment of a policy role at Middlesex University London, explains how to build the position in Chapter 12, "Punching above your weight: establishing a policy and public affairs function in a modern university". Exploring local influence, and building the concept of the "civic university", Selena Bolingbroke and Tess Winther provide a case study from Goldsmiths University of London in how the institution has developed its community presence in Chapter 13, "The influence of universities in a civic context". In the concluding essay, Chapter 14, "Influencing policy is core business for universities", Ant Bagshaw makes the case for seeing public affairs and policy engagement as a key component of university strategy and not as a peripheral activity.

The content of this book is not designed to be a simple recipe for how to establish or maintain a policy and public affairs function within a university, how to run a think-tank or lobbying organisation, or to set the priorities for civil servants or government ministers. This book provides ideas and recommendations for *how* to influence policy and an exploration of *why* that should happen. We hope that the book is a useful professional guide for colleagues across the HE sector.

Reference

Leach, M (2012, 19 January) Who let them in? *Times Higher Education*. Available from: www.timeshighereducation.com/features/who-let-them-in/418697.article

Concepts and theories for policy influence

CHAPTER 1

Power and influence in higher education policymaking

Who controls the debate?

Debbie McVitty

Introduction

Traditionally, policymaking – and higher education (HE) policymaking is no exception – has been a tightly controlled process, taking place within a well-defined circle of informed "insiders": those working in government departments, parliaments in London, Edinburgh, Cardiff, and Belfast, quangos, think-tanks, and formally constituted lobbying bodies. Laypeople typically rely on traditional media and specialist press to find out what policy is being made and how it might affect them and their organisations. Major policy set pieces such as independent reviews or government legislation include in their architecture the potential for the person on the street to express a view, and even have that view taken account of by decision-makers, but in practice the voices dominating the debate are the established insiders and professionals whose jobs require them to be policy-engaged. Academics interested in understanding the ebb and flow of power and influence in policymaking are typically required either to analyse public documentation or be granted this privileged insider status in their own right – and usually only well after the fact, when the key actors have moved into new roles, or retired.

All this may be true; it can legitimately be questioned whether it is right. The most recent calculation of the economic value of universities to the UK estimated the future benefits of research and development conducted in universities in a single year to be worth £28.9 billion to the UK economy, and the annual investment in students receiving their first degree to be £63 billion worth of increased human capital (Oxford Economics 2017). Universities support just under a million jobs and HE exports are worth £13.1 billion annually. Though universities are private organisations they receive public funding and there is a clear public interest in their operations. At a regional level, many different types of organisation depend on universities in different ways: to educate the professionals in teaching, social work, and health, to provide a flow of graduate-level skills into the economy, to provide innovation to business, and often to contribute to the local cultural and arts offer. Students and staff working and studying inside universities have a vested interest in their university's overall success and sustainability, and in the way external policy shapes the environment for research, teaching, and external engagement in their university. In other words, there are many stakeholders in HE who do not, as a rule, have much of a say in the policies that shape the sector.

Policy engagement is notionally far more accessible to interested laypeople, thanks to new digital technologies. The second decade of the twenty-first century will almost certainly be viewed from the perspective of history as the decade of social media. Facebook was opened up to the public in 2006 and in 2009 achieved 350 million registered users, becoming the largest social media platform in the world. Twitter was launched in 2006 and by 2012 had 100 million active users. At the most basic level, social media give individuals a voice and the capability to publish an opinion without the need for mediation, and allow the crowd to generate popular opinions and organise action using shares and likes.[1] In principle, social media ought to make policymaking more participative and democratic, with people empowered to have a greater say over issues that affect their lives and taking part in identifying issues, then proposing, and testing, solutions. In practice, social media can encourage us to create atomised echo-chambers, reinforcing established opinions and making us vulnerable to malign forces attempting to influence or harden our views.

Conventional media has always had an eye to the views of readers; it is notable that the kind of stories education journalists predominantly report tend to play to the anxieties of the middle classes. The implications are that: ordinary hard-working people are not getting enough access to elite universities because the privately educated or international students are taking up too many places; less-qualified students are lowering standards in universities; student debt may affect young people's ability to get a mortgage; and (if your newspaper of choice leans to the political right) universities are biased towards the liberal left. One effect of social media is that the mainstream media come under pressure to replicate the sense of immediacy and urgency that comes with social media, and to pursue shares and likes that will amplify the impact of journalism beyond a core group of readers or subscribers. Education journalists are not charlatans; they work hard to bring insight to their readers. But the contemporary media environment has low tolerance for complexity or nuance.

The second decade of the twenty-first century also saw a rise in political populism, with one in four Europeans estimated to have voted for a populist party, defined as a party claiming to represent the interests of the common people against those of an untrustworthy elite (Lewis et al. 2018). The UK Independence Party (UKIP) saw such a degree of success in the early part of the decade that it prompted the Prime Minister David Cameron to promise a referendum on the UK's membership of the EU, fearful that the Conservatives would lose ground to the UKIP threat in the 2015 General Election. Scottish nationalists dominate Scottish politics, and they were sufficiently powerful to command a referendum on Scottish independence in 2014. Following the 2015 General Election and the resignation of Labour leader Ed Miliband, left-wing radical Jeremy Corbyn swept to victory as Labour leader. It is well beyond the scope of this chapter to consider the causes of the populist turn in politics, but it is probably reasonable to argue that the 2008 global financial crisis, plus the 2009 MPs' expenses scandal, plus increasing social divisions generated by the period of economic austerity in the first half of the decade all played a role. Social media almost certainly fuelled the trend by enabling like-minded people holding opinions considered marginal to find each other, organise, and find support, and in helping to polarise political views.

As a result of the populist turn, even mainstream politicians are becoming increasingly adept at perceiving the emergence of an issue and claiming ownership of it, in order to win the approbation of the crowd. When Michael Gove said on Sky News during the referendum on the UK's future membership of the EU that "this country has had enough of experts" (Mance 2016) he captured a public mood that felt that an elite group had seized power and influence at the expense of ordinary people. Universities are especially vulnerable to being portrayed as elitist and complacent, pursuing their own interests at the expense of those of the country at large. Collectively, universities were supporters of the losing side in the EU referendum, and as such were challenged about how out of touch they were with their local communities (Matthews 2016). As Labour peer Andrew Adonis took to Twitter to point out to devastating effect in 2017, the heads of universities tend to enjoy comfortable remuneration (Heymann 2017). Moreover, compared to other public services, universities in England, at least, have been afforded a measure of protection from public sector cuts through the student fee system – an indicator of the influence university leaders wielded at the start of the decade. Crucially, universities have not been very effective at anticipating the populist turn and taking steps to protect themselves from attack. As a result, as Mark Leach has argued, the HE sector and its leadership are suffering "a collective crisis of moral authority, a crisis of leadership, and a crisis of identity" (Leach 2018).

For policy or public affairs professionals working in universities, the rules of the game – never especially well-defined to begin with – have changed beyond recognition in a matter of years. The intrusion of populism into HE policymaking tends to obscure, or squeeze out, genuine issues in favour of whipping up controversy. It is not surprising that universities, with their traditions of producing measured analysis and evidence, are nonplussed by this new world order. But if the university sector is unable to adapt, and unprepared to engage in ways which shape the policy environment, it will not survive in its current form for much longer. In an external environment shaped by populism and saturated by social media, meaningful engagement of stakeholders in policy development becomes not simply a matter of moral judgement but necessary for survival. Throughout the last decade, as I will argue in the next section, there has been a noticeable trend towards a populist approach in HE policymaking, with policymakers appealing directly to the public rather than working in collaboration with universities. Universities have been replaced by students as the objects and imagined beneficiaries of HE policymaking. The widespread inclusion of student representation in policymaking processes is a significant shift during this period. However, the effect of this populist appeal in policymaking has, in large measure, been to skew the debate towards controversy, rather than inform and empower the various HE stakeholders.

Policymaking in central government

In England, the primary source of HE reform in the last decade has been the government, through the 2011 White Paper, *Students at the heart of the system*, the 2015 Green Paper, *Fulfilling our potential*, and 2016 White Paper, *Success as a knowledge economy*, culminating in the Higher Education and Research Act 2017 (HERA). The two universities and science ministers primarily responsible for driving these policy agendas forward were David Willetts (2010–2014) and Jo Johnson (2015–2018), supported by their respective special advisors and senior civil servants. Although both ministers had a strong agenda to enhance university teaching quality, there was a noticeable difference in approach.

Willetts was a Conservative minister in a coalition government with the Liberal Democrats. This constrained his ability to put forward legislation to reform the sector, especially since the political fallout for the Liberal Democrats of the undergraduate fee reforms that saw the bulk of public funding to universities for teaching replaced with undergraduate student fees of up to £9,000 a year. Although aspects of Willetts's agenda were to make a *virtue* of fees – through encouraging HE to become more responsive to student choice and improve teaching quality (BIS 2011, 8) – the plans attracted significant criticism from some quarters (e.g. Collini 2011). On a number of occasions, Willetts demonstrated that he was an ally of the sector: for example, he commissioned evidence on the multiple benefits of HE across dimensions from individual to collective and from financial to social, and argued publicly and within government for the benefits of universities recruiting international students (Willetts 2013; 2014).

Jo Johnson held office across the 2015 and 2017 Conservative governments, a political leadership that became increasingly sceptical towards universities, especially following the outcome of the EU referendum in 2016 and the promotion of former Home Secretary Theresa May to Conservative party leader and Prime Minister. Between 2016 and 2017, Johnson oversaw the progress of the Higher Education and Research Bill (HERB) through the UK Parliament which established in law and practice an enhanced version of the Conservative agenda to foster teaching quality through stimulating competition. In a 2016 speech to Universities UK, Johnson called on the sector to collaborate with him on the passage of HERB (Johnson 2016). At the 2017 General Election the Conservative Party lost ground to Labour under the leadership of Jeremy Corbyn, whose flagship HE policy was the abolition of tuition fees. A marked shift in government tone towards universities followed. In 2017, addressing the Universities UK conference again, Johnson gave what he called a "realist critique" of HE focused on value for money for students, the risk of grade inflation, and the problem of excessive vice-chancellor pay (Johnson 2017). This hardening view towards universities inside the Westminster government is neatly encapsulated in a *Telegraph* article by former advisor to Theresa May, Nick Timothy, in which he argued that the university funding system was an "unsustainable and ultimately pointless Ponzi scheme" (Timothy 2017).

Government ministers and departments have a great deal of power to convene resources and attention around policy agendas, even outside the formal legislative process, and they are themselves influenced by changing priorities of central government and their reading of the mood of the public, especially through the media. Inside Parliament, however, behind the scenes, numerous actors attempt to influence and shape HE policy. Her Majesty's Opposition, individual MPs and peers, and government backbenchers can provide a constant stream of challenge through mechanisms such as written and oral questions to the Secretary of State, select committees, and the formal legislative process. The role of the Lords was instrumental in shaping the HERA, for example. Chapters 9 and 10 present detailed case studies of policies in the Welsh and Scottish contexts: each nation's government is powerful in the initiation of HE policy agendas.

Between universities and government: sector agencies and representative bodies

Representative bodies – Universities UK, Universities Scotland, Universities Wales, GuildHE for small and specialist providers, and Independent HE for "alternative" or "private" providers – exist to ensure that lobbying on behalf of universities is made more powerful by offering policymakers a combined voice. They exert influence through the publication of research and policy insight and through the media. In addition, MillionPlus, the Russell Group, and University Alliance are university "mission groups", representing member universities which feel they have something specific in common that gives them shared purpose outside the general role of representative bodies. They exert direct influence on policymakers through face-to-face meetings, the publication of reports and provision of commentary to the media. Think-tanks, such as the Institute for Public Policy Research, the Institute for Fiscal Studies, the New Economics Foundation, the Resolution Foundation, and the HE sector's designated think-tank, the Higher Education Policy Institute, feed a steady stream of ideas and insight into the debate. Although these reports are ostensibly public, they are primarily targeted at policymakers inside government.

Until 2018, the Higher Education Funding Council for England (Hefce) had a strong role in advising ministers on the development and implementation of policy, and so members of the funding council board, strategic advisory committees, and working groups – typically heads of institution or members of university senior teams – could leverage influence through those positions. Hefce had enormous policy agenda-convening power of its own, particularly through setting conditions and guidance associated with funding streams, such as the student opportunity funding provided to institutions in recognition of the costs of recruiting and supporting under-represented students. The Scottish Funding Council (SFC) and the Higher Education Funding Council for Wales (Hefcw) continue for the present to occupy a similar role in the Scottish and Welsh systems. Sector bodies such as the Quality Assurance Agency for Higher Education (QAA), the Office of the Independent Adjudicator for Higher Education in England and Wales (OIA), and the Higher Education Statistics Agency (HESA) can shape policy, given their responsibilities to enact it. Each of these bodies has its own power to convene a policy agenda; for example, QAA maintains a rolling review and development process of the UK Quality Code; the HESA Data Futures programme aims to update the sector's collection and handling of data, including the collection of data for regulatory purposes; and the OIA has initiated a programme of work on improving mechanisms for handling student complaints. The potential for different policy agendas to overlap means that the part of the HE sector that is concerned with policymaking has been obliged to maintain an enormous system of formal and informal meetings and events to make sure everyone is represented in everyone else's policymaking process. In fact, in addition to convening members to influence policy, representative bodies and mission groups have typically had a vital role in simply keeping universities informed about what is going on.

Notwithstanding that a large cast of individuals has been involved in shaping the development and implementation of HE policy, it remains accurate to say that this is a group of elite insiders and professional "policy wonks". Even the formal process of policy consultation, in which the relevant government department, agency, or organisation publishes its intentions and solicits views, though again, ostensibly a public-facing process, tends to engage those with professional responsibility for policy engagement. Policy consultation is a useful example of how there is a subset of policy influencers within the wider group of those who are professionally policy-engaged. Responding to policy consultations can take up significant time and effort within institutions; far better to be a member of the group or have the ear of the policymaker that is setting the consultation, as they rarely change significantly in light of the feedback received.

Since the replacement of Hefce with the Office for Students (OfS) in 2018 (a result of HERA), policymaking in England has become somewhat less collaborative. The switch could be characterised as a move from a funder to a regulator, but it is more accurately described as a switch from funding and co-regulation to pure regulation. Hefce regulated through attaching conditions to the funding it disbursed, particularly that universities should be well-managed, be financially sustainable, and engage with the regular assessment of their academic quality and standards. Hefce maintained close relationships with the providers it regulated, and its governance was predominantly made up of senior management in universities. Hefce's role was designed to mediate between government and universities, acting as an honest broker to encourage government to enact policy the sector could live with, and encouraging universities to respond to government policy agendas. The basis for Hefce's regulatory powers – public funding to universities – effectively ended with the increase of full-time undergraduate fees to £9,000, and the removal of the majority of the public subsidy to universities for teaching. Regulatory change was necessary to give a regulator the powers to regulate in its own right rather than on the basis of disbursal of funds. However, the shift to arm's-length pure regulation was more an ideological move than a technocratic one. It was felt within government that Hefce's deep knowledge of the universities it funded and regulated, and the degree of influence universities had in Hefce governance, amounted to "provider capture".

As a pure regulator, OfS has a statutory duty to prioritise the student interest, rather than the university interest, insofar as those interests do not overlap. In its early months of operation, it demonstrated to government ministers and the public that it was prepared to be tough on universities. As a result, it has tended to emphasise in its public narrative controversial issues like the pay of university leaders, grade inflation, student recruitment and admissions, freedom of speech, and its unwillingness to consider a bailout in the hypothetical situation that a university finds itself in financial trouble. Rather than quietly convening an influential group of university leaders, or commissioning experts, or working with representative bodies to generate a plan of action, OfS has tended to take to the media to express its concerns, for example in an announcement at the end of 2018 that universities should tackle "spiralling" grade inflation, which received widespread media coverage (OfS 2018). In one sense, this approach has brought HE policymaking to a broader audience; but, in another, it is presenting a very limited picture of the HE policy environment – and is arguably much less effective in generating action than a collaborative approach.

How student representatives became policy insiders

The naming of OfS signals the rise to prominence of students in HE policymaking in the last decade, as the objects and imagined beneficiaries, if not always the agents, of policy (see Chapter 6, by Adam Wright and Rille Raaper). As the national representative body for students in further and HE, the National Union of Students (NUS) has frequently been pulled in several different directions when it comes to deciding how it wants to influence policy agendas. The elected leadership is regularly obliged to pivot between attempting to spearhead a popular campaign through organising demonstrations or mass lobbies of decision-makers, and representing the student voice in closed meetings with ministers, civil servants, and the HE sector's leaders.

NUS is culturally committed to the principle of bringing student voices into policymaking; in that sense it is a force for democratisation in HE policymaking. But a pragmatic analysis of the nature of HE policymaking led NUS over the last decade to develop its policy insider status, consequently investing in its capacity to produce research and policy analysis, and playing a full role in the sector's policymaking processes. These efforts were aided considerably by government policy dating back to New Labour that sought to introduce student voices into policy, through mechanisms such as the National Student Survey (NSS) and, under the Coalition Government, to put students "at the heart of the system". Strong relationships between NUS and Hefce, QAA, OIA, and the Office for Fair Access (Offa) in particular have influenced policy, and have shaped a collective view of the value of incorporating student voices into policy discussions. As a consequence, the breadth of NUS's influencing work is not designed to be visible to students in general, though NUS, like other representative organisations, has undertaken work to keep its member students' unions informed and solicit their opinion on the policy environment.

NUS's hybrid insider/outsider status has created tensions. To be a policy insider makes an organisation complicit because effective insider policy influencing shapes interventions in light of the agendas and worldviews of those one is influencing. Outsider status can be advantageous for people who prefer to adopt a purist position and who consider that seeking a compromise or a small victory requires concession to a morally problematic premise. Put bluntly, there is no value in asking a Conservative government to cancel tuition fees, but there is probably a win to be gained on issues like loan repayment thresholds. Membership organisations are particularly vulnerable to accusations of selling out. This tension was exposed, ahead of a planned protest on tuition fees in 2010, when emails between NUS President Aaron Porter and policy officer Graeme Wise, and government special advisors in which NUS had argued for cuts to student grants as an alternative to a tuition fee increase, were leaked to the *Telegraph* (Kirkup, Prince, and Porter 2010).

University staff

The case of university staff is different from that of students: university staff representative bodies are trades unions and therefore focused more closely on pay and conditions than on policy influence and, unlike students, there has not been a concerted push to include staff voices in policymaking at the sector level, perhaps on the (problematic) assumption that these views can adequately be represented by those of the corporate university as expressed by institutional leaders. The trade union for many university academic and professional staff, the University and College Union (UCU), makes occasional policy interventions but, perhaps intentionally, has never achieved insider status – though its responses to the Green and White Papers on HE of 2015 and 2016 correctly identified the absence of the academic voice in the construction of the government's policy proposals (UCU 2016; 2017).

There is a school of thought that argues that confining policy development and debate to an insider group of professionals is the most efficient way to ensure that policy progresses with an appropriate degree of consultation. In this formulation, the vice-chancellor is trusted as an appropriate representative for the institution's interests, and registrars worry about compliance so that academics do not have to. Academics are, in a sense, protected from having to be concerned about policy issues and free to focus on teaching and research. The problem with this view is that academics are patently affected by the policy environment, both in the way their work is structured, and in the wider conceptualisation of the purpose of that work at institutional and national levels.

The potential emergent power of academics to shape the policy environment is demonstrated in the industrial action that took place in 2018 over proposed reforms to the Universities Superannuation Scheme (USS). A process that employers expected to be merely irksome exposed significant rifts inside universities between university leaders and staff. UCU found itself wrong-footed, as the force of negative feeling – amplified and extended on social media in ways that had not previously been seen – prompted rejection of a compromise deal that UCU leaders had negotiated with employers. The industrial action over USS had become a lightning rod for a wider mood of discontent and anger among university staff, who felt undervalued by, as they saw it, managerialist leaders who had lost sight of the value and purpose of HE. The issue of the USS valuation process and costs will continue to pose a policy challenge, probably for many years to come, but the real change arising from the USS industrial action of 2018 is likely to be that university leaders will be much more thoughtful about considering the limits of their power to control policy narratives in future.

Where could we go from here?

Populist politics and social media are clearly not going anywhere. Nor are they an unmitigated negative. Populism speaks to the desire for accountability; social media gives ordinary people a platform. The ability of policy insiders to open up policymaking, listen to diverse views, and adapt policy processes to include "outsiders" and enable them to have a meaningful stake could go a long way towards drawing the poison from the debate. Opening up the debate does not have to mean accommodating views that are ill-informed, or methodologically suspect, but it does require expanding the sorts of information that need to be taken account of in making policy. Expertise can, after all, be defined in many ways and found in many places. In the absence of a strong central entity with the convening power to create policy agendas and the reach to engage a wide diversity of voices, more organisations will need to take the initiative to start policy debates; the UPP Foundation's Civic University Commission is a good example of how cross-sector policy discussions can be had even in the absence of a central agency (McVitty 2019). A few universities have convened their own policy agendas: the 21st-Century Lab project at the University of Lincoln and the Industrial Strategy Commission convened jointly by the Universities of Manchester and Sheffield are fine examples.

Wonkhe has an important role to play in providing a platform for the public exchange of ideas based on the quality of the input rather than the status or role of the author. Mark Leach created Wonkhe in 2011 to be a "place that will allow the free exchange of ideas and opinion in an open and constructive way" (Leach 2011). Wonkhe was born out of a sense of frustration that there was limited debate within the sector over the Coalition Government's policies. Wonkhe is funded by a combination of institutional subscriptions to its daily briefing service and income from events and commercial partnerships, allowing it to maintain a free weekly briefing service and a website hosting debate and analysis of HE policy. For some the notion of a "wonk" implies insider status and expertise, but as Leach has explained, wonk is a term that implies being "smart, passionate, focused and engaged" and which can include anyone working in or interested in HE (Leach 2014). More than 35,000 individuals subscribe to Wonkhe's Monday Briefing, the majority of whom, one presumes, do not have "policy" in their job title. In 2019, Wonkhe launched WonkheSUs, a service targeted at students' unions to enable them to advocate for students' interests based on an informed understanding of the policy environment. Many of Wonkhe's current and former staff have experience of working in the national student movement, which could explain the democratic impulse that underpins the company. We are also insiders, with a professional background in policy analysis and influence.

The existence of Wonkhe won't save us, but it could be a good place to start. Inside universities, policy and public affairs professionals no longer have to spend a great deal of time educating themselves on the policy environment and explaining it to other people; Wonkhe does that for them. This means that the role can evolve to be significantly more strategic and externally engaged. Moreover, the notion of the corporate message vested in the person of the vice-chancellor can no longer be sustained. Policy ideas and insight may emerge from anywhere within the university, and from among the communities it serves. Wonkhe can be a vehicle to bring that insight into the public domain, but it will take universities thinking rather differently about policy influencing in the current political and communications landscape to take back ownership of the policy debate.

Note

1 A useful exploration of the impact of social media on changing how power and influence work is Jeremy Heimans and Henry Timms's *New Power: How Power Works in Our Hyperconnected World – And How to Make It Work for You* (2018). Heimans and Timms argue that to be able to influence and shape the world it is vital for leaders to understand and harness "new power" values and techniques, rooted in the participatory energy of the crowd and made possible by social technologies. Importantly, new power does not align with a political or moral position. New power practices such as crowdfunding and crowdsourcing ideas, and social movements that take place in the digital space such as #metoo and #blacklivesmatter, tap into the desire of people to participate.

References

BIS (2011) *Students at the Heart of the System*. London: Department for Business, Innovation and Skills.

Collini, S (2011, 25 August) From Robbins to McKinsey: the dismantling of the university. *London Review of Books*. Available from: www.lrb.co.uk/v33/n16/stefan-collini/from-robbins-to-mckinsey

Heimans, J and H Timms (2018) *New Power: How Power Works in Our Hyperconnected World – And How to Make It Work for You*. London: Penguin Random House.

Heymann, C (2017, 14 September) Six practical steps to deal with vice chancellor pay. *Wonkhe*. Available from: wonkhe.com/blogs/comment-reframe-vc-pay/

Johnson, J (2016, 8 September) *Universities UK Annual Conference 2016*. London: Department for Education. Available from: www.gov.uk/government/speeches/jo-johnson-universities-uk-annual-conference-2016

Johnson, J (2017, 7 September) *Speech to UUK Annual Conference*. London: Department for Education. Available from: www.gov.uk/government/speeches/jo-johnson-speech-to-uuk-annual-conference

Kirkup, J, R Prince and A Porter (2010, 8 December) National Union of Students secretly urged Government to make deep cuts in student grants. *The Telegraph*. Available from: www.telegraph.co.uk/education/universityeducation/8190379/National-Union-of-Students-secretly-urged-Government-to-make-deep-cuts-in-student-grants.html

Leach, M (2011, 31 January) What is Wonkhe? *Wonkhe*. Available from: wonkhe.com/blogs/what-is-wonkhe/

Leach, M (2014, 12 May) What is a wonk? *Wonkhe*. Available from: wonkhe.com/blogs/what-is-a-wonk/

Leach, M (2018, 9 March) The Enemy Within – why the narrative about universities and students went so wrong. *Wonkhe*. Available from: wonkhe.com/blogs/the-enemy-within-why-the-narrative-about-universities-and-students-went-so-wrong/

Lewis, P, S Clarke, C Barr, J Holder and N Kommenda (2018, 20 November) Revealed: one in four Europeans vote populist. *The Guardian*. Available from: www.theguardian.com/world/ng-interactive/2018/nov/20/revealed-one-in-four-europeans-vote-populist

Mance, H (2016, 3 June) Britain has had enough of experts, says Gove. *Financial Times*. Available from: www.ft.com/content/3be49734-29cb-11e6-83e4-abc22d5d108c

Matthews, D (2016, June 28) Brexit vote prompts academic soul-searching over gulf with public. *Times Higher Education*. Available from: www.timeshighereducation.com/news/brexit-vote-prompts-academic-soul-searching-over-gulf-public

McVitty, D (2019, 18 January) The Civic University Commission signals a new way of setting policy agendas. *Wonkhe*. Available from: wonkhe.com/blogs/the-civic-commission-signals-a-new-way-of-setting-policy-agendas/

OfS (2018, 19 December) *Universities Must Tackle 'Spiralling' Grade Inflation*. Bristol: Office for Students. Available from: www.officeforstudents.org.uk/news-blog-and-events/press-and-media/universities-must-tackle-spiralling-grade-inflation/

Oxford Economics (2017) *The Economic Impact of Universities in 2014–15*. London: Universities UK.

Timothy, N (2017, 17 August) Higher education has become unsustainable and young people know it. Radical change is the only solution. *The Telegraph*. Available from: www.telegraph.co.uk/news/2017/08/16/higher-education-has-become-unsustainable-young-people-know/

UCU (2016) *HE Green Paper*. London: University and College Union. Available from: www.ucu.org.uk/hegreenpaper

UCU (2017) *Higher Education White Paper 2016*. London: University and College Union. Available from: www.ucu.org.uk/article/8235/Higher-education-white-paper-2016

Willetts, D (2013) *Robbins Revisited: Bigger and Better Higher Education*. London: Social Market Foundation.

Willetts, D (2014, 23 December) May's mean spirited plan will damage Britain. *The Times*. Available from: www.thetimes.co.uk/article/mays-mean-spirited-plan-will-damage-britain-8ks0spkwv55

CHAPTER 2

Preparing for politics with a capital P

Josie Cluer and Sean Byrne

Introduction

Much "wonkery" focuses on detailed, rational policy analysis. But those who seek to influence policy need to influence policymakers. And some of them – arguably the most important ones – inhabit the political sphere too. They are Members of Parliament, ministers, special advisers, and party staffers. The world of politics is wider and messier than the world of policy. It needs to understand and take account of how people feel, what makes people angry, what people think is fair, and the political machines – parties, parliament, elections – that drive how things get done in running the country. When wonks work with ministers and other politicians, they usually do well on the policy side, but are less effective at understanding, and therefore responding to, the political side. This chapter attempts to explain why politics is important to Higher Education (HE) wonks, and argues that it will become increasingly so over the next decade. It offers a potted history of the HE debates that have hit the big time in political public discourse and analyses the factors that have turned a policy discussion into a political one. It looks to the future to outline some issues which are likely to attract public and media attention. Last, it offers some advice to wonks about how to influence politics as well as policy.

Part one: why should HE's wonks care about politics?

Britain is a democracy. That means that the people who ultimately run the country (ministers) and make our laws (Members of Parliament) are part of a political system which is underpinned by elections, party politics, and public opinion. These things matter in the policymaking process. And the less decision-makers know about policy, the more politics matters.

So how do you know an issue has broken from only a policy issue to a political issue? Some tell-tale signs: the newspaper front pages splash on it, BBC Radio 4's Today programme talks about it, radio phone-ins have angry people calling about it, Twitter has a storm about it, Facebook has people sharing GIFs about it, friends have angry and emotional conversations at dinner about it, others write to their MP about it, MPs ask parliamentary questions about it and debate it, parties clash on it, opinion pollsters ask people what they think about it, and local party branch meetings have motions about it. So far, so democratic. But, sometimes, politics gets ugly. For some reason or another, an issue finds its way into the limelight in a way that is high-risk for the sector involved. This is what we call "the danger zone". In this zone, the issue concerned is so controversial that it *dominates* public discourse. It generates so much anger and interest that policy decisions are made without clear heads. Decisions are less likely to be underpinned by detailed policy analysis. Things move fast, and results can be unpredictable. There is sometimes damage done to the reputations of the sector, institutions, or people involved. Generally, one does not want to be in the danger zone. HE in particular wants to avoid it because its success relies upon a strong reputation, long-term funding, stability, and the predictability of the policy environment.

The first two decades of the twenty-first century have been a relatively benign political climate for HE. By any comparison, politics has been kind to HE. The sector has stayed low on the public's worry list and mostly out of the headlines (YouGov 2018). On the big issues like funding and institutional autonomy, it has enjoyed a degree of political consensus that other public services might only dream of. Such consensus has been driven by shared beliefs between the two major political parties in Westminster. The first belief is a diagnosis about how Britain competes amidst the constraints of a knowledge-based, globalising economy, where Britain succeeds because it is an international hub of ideas, trade, and, above all, skills. As Gordon Brown put it in his last party conference speech as Chancellor:

> Strip away the rhetoric about globalisation and it comes down to one essential truth: You can buy raw materials from anywhere, You can borrow capital from anywhere, You can engage with technology way across the world, But you cannot buy from elsewhere what in the global economy you need most; the skills and the creativity of all our people - and that means that in education we must aim to be number one.
>
> (Brown 2006)

A decade letter, George Osborne framed education by saying:

> It's also the single most important thing we can do to boost the long-term productivity of our economy, because our nation's productivity is no more and no less than the combined talents and efforts of the people of these islands.
>
> (Weale 2016)

George Osborne applied the same principles to his decision to remove the cap on HE student numbers, arguing that: "Access to higher education is a basic tenet of economic success in the global race" (Morgan 2013).

The second belief is about the role of the state itself – about what it can and should do – as a steward of the nation's prosperity. Economic policy for UK governments in recent decades has focused on the productivity of the supply side of the economy, which in HE has prioritised policies to tackle market failures that disrupt the development and availability of skills. Neither side has seen it as their job to define what skills the nation actually needs for the kind of society and economy it wants to have, or define where these are to come from or how they are to be applied. With both parties framing the sector in similar terms like this, the major debates have been about policy but not much politics. The impact of this low profile has been profound. In one of the longest periods of public spending constraint for a century (the 2010 Coalition Government's "austerity" policy), funding from tuition fees and grants had more than doubled to around £10bn in England by 2015. The sector accelerated its expansion of a traditional degree model just when deep cuts in day-to-day spending forced many other public services fundamentally to redesign what they do, and how they do less of it. While the health service, for example, was reorganised under Major's government, Blair's government (twice), and Cameron's government, HE in England is only coming to see a new regulatory regime through the Higher Education and Research Act of 2017.

Part two: the danger zone in the past

There have been, of course, some political controversies for HE. This section will look at HE issues that have entered the danger zone in the years since the mid-2000s and will explore why. We will look at various factors that can push the sector into this zone:

1. **Touching a public nerve** – underlying divisions in public opinion that generate strong feelings. These tend to be anything on class, race, or gender, or issues like abortion, the death penalty, and morality.
2. **Prevailing political winds** – the underlying political narratives which, if a policy issue plays into them, could be amplified or accelerated into the danger zone, of which a new period of populism and distrust of "elite" institutions is currently by far the most dramatic (Leach 2018).
3. **Issues of the day** – big political issues which cut across all sectors, and have applicability to HE (Brexit, for example).
4. **The echo effect** – when an issue has similarities to another huge controversy of the past. Reopening the debate, or moving into the same space, can cause real trouble. This is why no government has tried to reform the

way we pay our council tax – the poll tax casts such a heavy shadow over politics that no government has dared go near it.

5. **Electoral, parliamentary or party politics** – these are issues which have such importance to the electoral maths that politicians have to take a particular view. For example, the "triple lock" on pensions has been promised by all parties for years, in no small part because the over 65s have the highest voter turnout amongst any group.

Politics is complex and, in many cases, a number of these factors are in play. So, how have these driven HE into the danger zone?

Access – touching a nerve

Admission to university – particularly to the most selective institutions – has always been a hot topic in the UK. It always will be. Here we conflate "fair access" (i.e. access to those most selective universities) and "widening participation" (i.e. access to higher education). This is because the same fundamental societal trends and beliefs underpin the debate surrounding both. Though we note that the public debate – led as it is by politicians and journalists who hugely over-represent the most selective universities – is particularly interested in the fair access issue, and indeed the examples which have entered the "danger zone" are more about access to "elite" universities rather than the transformative education at the less selective end of the sector.

Laura Spence was the northern sixth former who applied to the University of Oxford to study medicine and was rejected; either because she was educated at a state school, in Gordon Brown's view (BBC 2000a), or because others were better qualified, in Oxford's view (BBC 2000b). This was not a policy debate about how to reduce the dependence of Oxbridge on privately educated students, or how to make sure selective procedures were fair on students, or the subtleties of the balance of responsibility between schools, colleges, and universities in driving social mobility. Instead, the ingredients of "Oxbridge" (which accounts for 2% of undergraduate students, but a vastly greater proportion of column inches on HE) – elitism, class, and education – elevated the debate to the front pages for over a week. Trevor Phillips took up the access mantle in 2003, arguing against the University of Bristol's contextual data policy to widen access, and some independent schools even boycotted institutions which were seen to "go too far" in this regard (Macleod 2003). David Lammy MP has taken up the access issue from the perspective of race, establishing from Freedom of Information Act requests that in one year, ten Oxford colleges and six Cambridge colleges did not award a place to a black British pupil with A-levels (Adams and Bengtsson 2017). We could go on.

Why is access such a hot topic? It is partly because class is such an important part of British social life: the Government's Social Mobility Commission
found that around half of people (48%) believe that where you end up in
society today is mainly determined by your background and who your parents are (Social Mobility Commission 2017). It goes to the heart of political
debate in the UK: social mobility, social justice, fairness, equality, class, elitism, aspiration, race, and discrimination. All these concepts provoke strong
reactions. Further (and perhaps because of this), all the major political parties have education, and its power to drive social mobility, as a core belief
and an inherent part of their histories and narratives. Institutions like The
Open University and Ruskin College have an iconic place in Labour's self-
image (echoed in proposals in Labour's 2017 election manifesto for a National
Education Service intended to make "education a right, not a privilege") and
the appeal of a society where people flourish through their own hard work
and merit is a leitmotif of British politics – from the image of Thatcher as the
"grocer's daughter" from Grantham who made it to Oxford to study chem-
istry, to Miliband's "promise of Britain", David Cameron's commitment that
"for us Conservatives, the party of aspiration … we know that education is
the springboard to opportunity" (*Independent* 2015), and Theresa May's commitment on the steps of Downing Street to fight "burning injustice" and "to
do everything we can to help anybody, whatever your background, to go as
far as your talents will take you" (May 2016).

This is amplified by the personal stories and experiences of politicians of
all stripes. Just think how many politicians talk not just about being "the first
in their family to go to university" but how the opportunities it gave them
have transformed their lives, and how important it is to them and their politics. As we will see below, "access" is the vortex issue of HE; it is so fundamental to how society and politicians think about HE that it sucks in all other
debates and discussions.

Fees, take one: 2003/4 – touching a nerve and prevailing political winds

The nuts and bolts of the fees discussion in the HE sector is all about policy:
if, as a country, we expand HE then we need to fund it. In 2003,[1] without a
huge injection of cash, the financial sustainability of universities was at risk,
not to mention the quality of teaching and staff pay. The issue was blown into
the danger zone by two factors: the access issue outlined above and prevailing political winds. First, access acted as the vortex issue. Debates about who
should pay for HE were a proxy for debates about social mobility, fairness,
and "whose side you were on". The governing Labour Party felt deeply uneasy
about asking students to pay for their education; the power of education to

transform lives and power social mobility is deeply ingrained in the Labour party, and to do anything to limit access for people who were less well-off was the antithesis to everything many Labour politicians and party members came into politics to do. Second, in the 2001 election, the Labour Party's manifesto was clear that Labour "will not introduce 'top-up' fees and has legislated to prevent them" (Labour 2001). In 2003/4, the education secretary introduced the Higher Education White Paper which introduced variable tuition fees of up to £3,000. This did not play well with voters or MPs who were already fed up with a Prime Minister seen as "Bliar" and famous for "spin over substance". The fees issue dominated front pages, radio talk shows, family discussions, and water-cooler conversations. Constituency parties held votes about deselecting their MPs. The parliamentary vote saw Blair's biggest backbench revolt, with the Government securing the change by just five votes.

Fees, take two: the echo effect, prevailing political winds, and touching a nerve (again)

During the Coalition Government, the policy debate was almost a re-run of the 2003/4 debate, and the political debate had similar factors. The echo effect from 2003/4 loomed large. Labour in particular remembered the pain of the fees debate, the impact on their majority in 2005, and the political price they paid. The Conservatives were not pain free, remembering that three MPs defied their whips in 2004 and they were opposed to the policy. The prevailing political wind was a narrative that the Liberal Democrats had "sold out" their principles for power, and that Deputy Prime Minister and leader of the Liberal Democrats Nick Clegg was Pinocchio, a puppet played by his master, Prime Minister David Cameron. In the 2010 election, the Lib Dems had made a commitment to oppose tuition fees. Many MPs had made the pledge publicly, with pictures and placards, which were perfect images to be thrown back at them. No matter that pre-2010, no one thought the Lib Dems would be in power, nor that the leadership had been very clearly against the party policy, which Nick Clegg regarded as unaffordable, which had been imposed upon it by the Lib Dem party conference (Watt 2009). No matter that the country had a huge deficit and the political consensus was to restrain public spending. As per the previous fees debate, the policy nuance – about the affordability of world-class universities, of the repayment threshold versus the interest rate versus the fee rate – was lost. As Clegg himself says, it all played into a narrative about how the Lib Dems had sold out by getting into bed with the Tories (Clegg 2016). In the end, Clegg apologised for making a promise he couldn't keep but the damage was done, and the apology is now better remembered for the viral YouTube video it created. The Lib Dems suffered electoral disaster in 2015.

Vice-chancellors' pay: issue of the day

Vice-chancellors' (VC) pay is a useful more recent example of the issue-of-the-day risk; the issue being "fat cat" pay. The combination of the banking crisis, rising inequality between workers and executives, wage stagnation, and the gender pay gap has seen concern about income inequality increase. This is not just an HE issue, not just one for policy wonks in the sector, but an issue of the day. It cuts across business, government departments, and, somewhat unexpectedly, VCs. It was ultimately responsible for the University of Bath VC's resignation (Coughlan 2017), and a series of uncomfortable moments for other VCs across the sector. The sector was not ready for the VC pay issue to explode, and it was slow to respond. When it did, it did so with incredulity that it was an issue (Heymann 2017). The sector so misdiagnosed the problem that it turned up to a gunfight with a casserole, not acknowledging that this is a political question as much as a policy one. This is damaging to the sector, because it allowed itself to be characterised alongside "fat cats" rather than – more positively – alongside other engines of social mobility.

Part three: the future

The issues described above are the danger-zone issues, but the factors that push them there play out at a less dramatic level week in, week out. Over the coming months and years, the debates wonks will find themselves in are increasingly political for three reasons. First, the electoral arithmetic is tighter than it has been in many years. The 2017 government's power depended on a minor party (the Northern Irish Democratic Unionist Party) for confidence and supply. In this context, all issues dealt with in and by parliament are more likely to become subject to political factors. Second, politics is becoming increasingly polarised. Political debate has become more oppositional since 2015, and not just in the UK. The polarisation of politics in Europe and the Americas, and demonstrated so spectacularly by Brexit, is a "new normal". The days of politicians squabbling over the centre ground are gone. Politics is angrier and nastier too. It is now not uncommon for establishment figures to "troll" each other on social media. This means that for HE, we cannot rely upon the consensus about its role, funding and value which has benefited the sector in the past. In a world where the consensus described earlier about the essential role of universities in the economic and social progress of the UK could break down, the sector may find itself needing to make the case for its very existence, which has not previously been in question. Third, HE needs policymakers now more than ever. As described earlier, in the old world, HE's plea to government was basically "keep students coming to university, keep the science ringfenced, and leave us to it". The odd barter aside (on access, research priorities, and innovation in courses), government largely complied. In this new world, the sector is going to need government to intervene more than before, particularly to help manage loss of access to European research collaborations and funding and to sustain the flow of international students (and academics) into UK universities who are so critical not just for funding but for universities' richness and culture. In a post-Brexit world, with the rise of universities all over the world (particularly in anglophone markets like Australia and Canada, but also in China, the Middle East, and Latin America), HE needs government policy to help to continue this flow.

In this more volatile and more divergent political context where HE needs politicians more than ever before, what are the prevailing political winds and the issues of the day HE wonks need to consider? The themes shaping public debate have changed and are more likely to impact on HE than before. Michael Gove's "we've had enough of experts" jibe has encapsulated a new era of public discourse where being factually incorrect is no longer a bar to public credibility, and having spent a career researching a topic does not necessarily make people more likely to listen to you (in fact, sometimes quite the opposite). This **prevailing political wind** is the most dangerous for universities because it challenges their fundamental purpose – furthering human knowledge, using education to build better societies and establishing how the world works. Universities have been slow to react to this shift in public attitude; with some notable exceptions, the defence of fact-based discourse and the role of expertise is being led by journalists (like Full Fact) and charities (like Sense about Science).

A similar and related political wind is virulently anti-establishment. The criticisms of "the mainstream media" the "Westminster bubble" and the "metropolitan liberal elite" rail against the institutions and norms which have dominated politics and society for generations. In many ways, universities, with their rigorous challenge of ideas and thinking, could be a perfect antidote to the establishment. But as Andrew Adonis has shown, it is too easy for the sector to be presented as an establishment itself (Parr 2017). The **issues of the day** are already providing challenges for HE. Wonks need to be ready. #metoo is a worldwide movement which has reached into politics, Hollywood, and business, unseating established figures and challenging the acceptability of old norms. Universities have not been immune, but it is likely that there will be more to come. Similarly, the importance of mental health, LGBTQ rights, and gender pay all require thoughtful and proactive responses. The **echo effect** will come into play soon. The 2017 Conservative government's post-18 funding review and yet another discussion on fees will reopen old wounds. And, of course, it will all be seen through the class/social mobility/fairness lens, with the added anti-establishment kicker. It remains to be seen whether this time around, the political debate sees a more fundamental difference opening up about the expansion, value, and purpose of higher education.

The party-political context provides an interesting backdrop to the politics of HE. In the analysis of voting habits, age is the new class: a fundamental indicator of voting intention is age. Younger voters strongly favour Labour while older voters strongly favour Conservatives with the crossover point around 50 years old (Ipsos Mori 2017). Of course, not all students are young, and not all young people are students, but these numbers have not been lost on either main party, as shown by both parties in the 2017 General Election and its aftermath wooing young voters with policies around reducing (May) or scrapping (Corbyn) fees.

But voting habits are just one part of the story. There is a prevailing political wind too: a whole generation of young people feel they are the first generation to do worse than their parents did. Indeed, David Willetts's *The Pinch* argues that the baby boomers had it all – free education, the summer of love, gold-plated pensions, cheap houses that increased 10 to 20 times in value – leaving the millennials to clean up the mess (Willetts 2010). This generation sees themselves facing student debt of £50k+ with an accompanying eye-watering interest rate of 6 per cent, a housing ladder that starts way above their heads, and the expectation they will work till they're at least 70. Worse, the baby boomers voted for Brexit, which will make the millennials poorer and their country less powerful. To add insult to injury, (baby boomer) government ministers complain millennials eat too much avocado and drink too many flat whites. The true picture may be less black and white, but the generational divide is real. It is no wonder that young people are voting like they never have before (Sturgis and Jennings 2018) and asking themselves what they are getting for their money. This trend impacts HE both because HE is seen as the home for young people, and because HE is more expensive. Now, more than ever, HE needs an answer to the questions of "What do I get for my money?" and "Is it worth it?"

Part four: what should wonks do about it?

As we've seen, politics is an important part of the policy ecosystem. Increasingly so. What does this mean for wonks, those people working in and around HE policy?

1) Understand it

First and most importantly, wonks need to understand the political arena and its likely impact on the policy system. Wonks should familiarise themselves with the political system: everything from how parliament works to the party system and the mechanics of elections. Read the political news, listen to the podcasts, see what people are talking about on Twitter, have a flick through the political gossip columns to understand who's on the way up and down, talk to political nerds and political activists. It's also worth understanding a bit about polling, public opinion, and voting patterns, and reading the "commentariat" views – commentators, columnists, and bloggers. For those who get carried away, the party websites (ConservativeHome, LabourList, LibDemVoice) provide great insight into the party machines and the pressures politicians are under from their parties, and partisan think-thanks provide interesting thinking which may influence party policy.

2) Predict it

Wonks should think about the winds blowing through political and public discourse and think about which HE discussions could get caught up in them. How could the issues of the day draw universities in? What discussions are you entering into which have a painful past for politicians (or subsets of them)? What are the political circumstances that are affecting a particular politician that might influence their view on the policy position? This could include personal issues like where they grew up, went (or did not go) to university, what their parents did and whether they went to university. It could include constituency issues like the size of their majority, whether there is a university in their constituency, whether students or young people are likely to be a key part of their electorate. It could include more party-political considerations like whether they are trying to get promoted (and therefore more likely to be loyal) or not, whether they hold office or not (in government, parliament or the party), and what their personal style is (a campaigning MP or a wonkish MP). All of these factors will play into how wonks should prepare for and engage with politicians.

3) Roll with it

It's very easy for wonks – with their rational policy analysis and reason – to get frustrated with the political system, and the challenges it poses. One response is to try to change it, but to do so, one needs to enter the political fray. Instead, it is better to roll with it. It is what it is: the job of the wonk is not to change it but to influence it.

4) Be ready for it

Last, a challenge to the sector. If we agree that politics is getting more prominent, more volatile, and moving faster, the sector should be asking itself how ready it is to respond to ending up in the danger zone. Is it quick enough to realise the challenges? Is it media savvy enough to navigate the press? Is it coordinated enough to respond strategically to protect not just individual institutions but the sector? Is it politically well-connected enough to get the support it needs? Should that response come from individual universities, sector bodies or the mission groups? We are not sure. But we do know that if the sector finds itself in the danger zone again, it will want to be ready to navigate it.

Conclusion

Policy has always been shaped and guided by politics, driven by deeply held beliefs about social mobility and fairness, painful political debates of the past, the political narratives of the day, and, of course, the party-political machine. Recent political trends give reason to believe that politics will be more polarised and more unpredictable than in the days of squabbling over the centre ground. This is even more true in HE, a policy area in which a previous consensus seems to be dissolving. HE wonks need to be ready for this extra injection of politics in their policy debates. Only by understanding, predicting, and being ready for the Politics – with a capital P – will they be able to influence the policies that will support the sector to thrive.

Note

1 The fees debate actually goes back to John Major's government, which commissioned Ron Dearing to review higher education funding. Both the policy and politics do not change much through the years, so we use 2003 as the case study.

References

Adams, R and H Bengtsson (2017, 19 October) Oxford accused of "social apartheid" as colleges admit no black students. *The Guardian*. Available from: www.theguardian.com/education/2017/oct/19/oxford-accused-of-social-apartheid-as-colleges-admit-no-black-students

BBC (2000a, 26 May) Chancellor attacks Oxford admissions. *BBC News*. Available from: news.bbc.co.uk/1/hi/education/764141.stm

BBC (2000b, 1 June) Oxford professor's fury at government. *BBC News*. Available from: news.bbc.co.uk/1/hi/education/772716.stm

Brown, G (2006, 25 September) In full: Gordon Brown's speech. *BBC News*. Available from: news.bbc.co.uk/1/hi/uk_politics/5378312.stm

Clegg, N (2016) *Politics: Between the Extremes*. London: Bodley Head.

Coughlan, S (2017, 29 November) University of Bath vice-chancellor quits in pay row. *BBC News*. Available from: www.bbc.co.uk/news/education-42152743

Heymann, C (2017, 14 September) Six practical steps to deal with vice chancellor pay. *Wonkhe*. Available from: wonkhe.com/blogs/comment-reframe-vc-pay/

Independent (2015, 7 October) Tory Party Conference 2015: David Cameron's speech in full. *The Independent*. Available from: www.independent.co.uk/news/uk/politics/tory-party-conference-2015-david-camerons-speech-in-full-a6684656.html

Ipsos MORI (2017, 20 June) How Britain voted in the 2017 election. Available from: www.ipsos.com/ipsos-mori/en-uk/how-britain-voted-2017-election

Labour (2001) *2001 Labour Party General Election Manifesto*. Available from: labourmanifesto.com/2001/2001-labour-manifesto.shtml

Leach, M (2018, 9 March) The Enemy Within – why the narrative about universities and students went so wrong. *Wonkhe*. Available from: wonkhe.com/blogs/the-enemy-within-why-the-narrative-about-universities-and-students-went-so-wrong/

Macleod, D (2003, 10 March) Bristol rebuts bias claims by CRE head. *The Guardian*. Available from: www.theguardian.com/education/2003/mar/10/highereducation.accesstouniversity

May, T (2016, 13 June) *Statement from the New Prime Minister Theresa May*. Available from: www.gov.uk/government/speeches/statement-from-the-new-prime-minister-theresa-may

Morgan, J (2013, 5 December) Undergraduate numbers cap "to be abolished" – Osborne. *Times Higher Education*. Available from: www.timeshighereducation.com/news/undergraduate-numbers-cap-to-be-abolished-osborne/2009667.article

Parr, C (2017. June 13) Andrew Adonis hits out at academics (and academics hit back). *Times Higher Education*. Available from: www.timeshighereducation.com/blog/andrew-adonis-hits-out-academics-and-academics-hit-back

Social Mobility Commission (2017, 15 June) *Social Mobility Barometer Poll*. Available from: https://www.gov.uk/government/publications/social-mobility-barometer-poll

Sturgis, P and W Jennings (2018, 6 December) Why 2017 may have witnessed a Youthquake after all. *LSE British Policy and Politics*. Available from: blogs.lse.ac.uk/politicsandpolicy/was-there-a-youthquake-after-all/

Watt, N (2009, 20 September) Nick Clegg faces backlash over weakened pledge on university fees. *The Guardian*. Available from: www.theguardian.com/politics/2009/sep/20/nick-clegg-tuition-fees-education

Weale, S (2016, 16 March) Osborne considers compulsory maths lessons for under-18s. *The Guardian*. Available from: www.theguardian.com/uk-news/2016/mar/16/osborne-budget-compulsory-maths-lessons-under-18s-student-children-schools

Willetts, D (2010) *The Pinch: How the Baby Boomers Took Their Children's Future – And Why They Should Give It Back*. London: Atlantic Books.

YouGov (2018) *Top Issues Tracker (GB)*. Available from: yougov.co.uk/topics/political-trackers/survey-results

CHAPTER 3

Evidence and policy

Theoretical approaches for higher education policymaking

Anna Bradshaw and Megan Dunn

Introduction

The higher education (HE) policymaking process in the UK does not always work as well as one might want. Politicians, civil servants, expert practitioners, and academic researchers ignore one another and talk at cross purposes. This has been one of the few things that has felt constant to us across the variety of roles we have held, from students' unions (where we both started) to national membership organisations, learned societies, expert agencies, and government departments. When caught up in the middle of the policymaking process – whether that's as someone generating policy ideas, someone seeking to influence policymakers, or someone making decisions – it can be hard to find the time to step back and think about why this is so.

In this chapter, we try to take this step back, and to think about one of the places in which the policymaking process can go wrong: the relationship between evidence and policy. We build on two main starting points. One is our experiences of working in the HE sector and taking part in some of its most heated debates. The other is an article by Christina Boswell and Katherine Smith, "Rethinking policy 'impact': four models of research policy relations" (2017). They outline four key approaches to thinking about the relationship between research and policy, which in this chapter we broaden, to consider evidence more generally, and narrow, to focus on HE. The structure of this chapter owes a significant debt to their article and we highly recommend it to anyone interested in research impact, or in a more thorough treatment of the theoretical approaches we describe. Following Boswell and Smith, we identify four key approaches to theorising the relationship between evidence and policy impact:

1. Evidence shapes policy
2. Policy shapes evidence
3. Co-production
4. Autonomous spheres

This chapter will describe each of these four approaches and relate them to real-life examples of HE policymaking in the UK, ranging from traditionally wonky policy areas like the Research Excellence Framework (REF) and the removal of student number caps to more topical questions of free speech on campus and the outsized clout of the alumni of the Universities of Oxford and Cambridge in politics and policymaking. We aim through this approach to demonstrate the importance of taking some time to step back from the day-to-day activity of policymaking, reflecting on the kind of relationship that we would like to see between evidence and policy, and how we can make that relationship happen.

Approach one: "evidence shapes policy"

The idea that policy should in some way be based on evidence is in many ways the cornerstone of "good" policymaking in many sectors, including in HE. Developing "evidence-based policy" has been an official priority of the UK Government for 20 years, since the commitment to making "better use of evidence and research in policy making" in the Modernising Government White Paper (Cabinet Office 1999; Stevens 2011; Wyatt 2002). While initially a project of Tony Blair's Labour government, this approach has persisted through governments of different political orientations (Wyatt 2002; Stevens 2011; Cabinet Office 2013). A commitment to evidence-based policy can currently be seen in the Civil Service's "Policy Lab" and "Open Policy Making" and many government departments have mechanisms in place for using evidence in their policymaking (Policy Lab 2018; Sasse and Haddon 2018). This ongoing government commitment has coincided with the growth of a group of organisations committed to coordinating and building the evidence base for evidence-based policy, including the Cochrane Collaboration from 1993, the National Institute of Health and Social Care from 1999, the Campbell Collaboration from 1999, and the Alliance for Useful Evidence from 2011.

The classical formulation of this approach to evidence and policy sees the relationship in terms of a linear sequence moving from basic research, through applied research and development, to application (Weiss 1979, 427). While more nuanced, complicated versions of this approach have since been developed, it is this simple, linear formulation that has "become increasingly embedded within UK policy" (Boswell and Smith 2017, 3). The official commitments to using evidence in this way have led to a significant number of (largely unfavourable) appraisals of whether government is succeeding in this commitment (Boswell and Smith 2017; Stevens 2007; Stevens 2011; Naughton 2005). Among the more nuanced versions of the "evidence shapes policy" approach is Weiss' "enlightenment" model, whereby the main route through which social science research affects policy is via the "concepts and theoretical perspectives" that "permeate the policy-making process" (Weiss 1979, 429; Weiss 1977). This "comforting" model suggests that researchers do not need to speak directly to live policy problems, but instead can get on with research in the knowledge that "without any special effort, truth will triumph" through a diffuse process (Weiss 1979, 430). Weiss herself is critical of what this model might mean for the relationship between evidence and policy, given its inefficiency and its vulnerability to "oversimplification and distortion" (ibid.). However, while both the linear and enlightenment formulations of this model have been criticised, they continue to be extremely influential. In fact, this approach underpins the "impact" agenda in UK research funding, including the REF's research impact case studies and the importance of "pathways to impact" in applications for funding from the UK research councils, which require researchers to demonstrate that their research has achieved identifiable, measurable influence beyond academia (Boswell and Smith 2017, 2; REF 2011; REF 2017). This emphasis on direct, linear impact is also felt in the routes taken by evidence sought when government is making policy *about* HE.

Student number controls

In December 2013, then-Chancellor George Osborne used the Autumn Statement to announce that the Government would be lifting the cap on student number controls, in the first instance by 30,000 places, and then, after a year, entirely. This news came as a surprise to the HE sector, which had resigned itself to having lost the argument for a mass HE system (Westwood 2013). The policy was announced in three sentences, and yet still George Osborne found space to reference the evidence base from which the policy came. Its basis, according to the Chancellor, was that each year 60,000 young people, who were qualified for and wanted to study in UK universities, were "prevented from doing so because of an arbitrary cap" (HC Deb 2013). While it was not made clear where this number was quoted from, it is possible that it was taken from a UCAS admissions process review in 2011, which found that at the end of the 2010 cycle 63,000 applicants who had declined offers were unplaced (UCAS 2011, 18). In a 2014 Higher Education Policy Institute (HEPI) briefing, Nick Hillman, previously special advisor to David Willetts (Universities Minister 2010–2014), expanded on the reasoning given by George Osborne: "HM Treasury recognise that delivering more higher-level skills is one of the most effective levers for delivering economic growth" (Hillman 2014). While the effect and impact of the removal of student number controls were and, certainly in the long term, remain unknown, those involved in the policymaking process seem keen to emphasise that evidence was gathered in order to drive the policy outcome.

Approach two: "policy shapes evidence"

One of the most significant critiques of the "evidence shapes policy" approach is that it ignores the ways in which policy, politics, and power shape evidence. As Boswell and Smith point out, there is a "rich body of literature" that theorises how politics and power shape the creation of knowledge, expertise, and academic authority, including the work of Foucault and Gramsci (Boswell and Smith 2017, 4). What these theoretical contributions have in common is an emphasis on how the creation and use of evidence are fundamentally motivated by politics (ibid.). Even without landing on any particular theoretical interpretation, taking this approach can require an appreciation of the fact that deciding what counts as evidence is in itself a politically loaded discussion (Nutley, Walter, and Davies 2007 in: Stevens 2011, 238; Bailey and Scott-Jones 1984). There is some empirical evidence of the impact of policy and politics on evidence, though perhaps less than might be expected (Hill 2009 in: Stevens 2011, 237–238; Nutley et al. 2007, 2). One helpful and fairly recent example comes from Stevens (2011). In his study of the use of evidence in one government department in 2009, he finds that even among a team of civil servants who are committed to using evidence in their policymaking, the need to tell "policy stories" that fit with a prevailing approaches, and the need to demonstrate bureaucratic competence, can "short-circuit" the commitment to using evidence well (Stevens 2011, 251).

In HE policy, politics can shape the formation of evidence by an even more direct route: policy *about* research. When government is a major source of funding for academic research, it has significant power over the kinds of research that are possible.

The Research Excellence Framework (REF)

In the UK, government funding of research reaches researchers through two routes (the "dual support" system): competitive grant funding for particular projects, and "long-term, stable" block grants provided to institutions on the basis of "quality" (Stern 2016, 6). This quality-related (QR) funding is explicitly intended to support research independence, and therefore is likely to be the portion of government research funding that is the least likely to restrict the kinds of research that are possible (Research England n.d.). However, the mechanism by which the quality of research is judged, the REF, has come under meaningful criticism. For example, The Royal Society notes that "the REF is widely blamed for creating perverse incentives in the research system" (The Royal Society 2017). In his review of the research funding system in 2016, Nicholas Stern found that the "desire to be included in the REF, and associated pressures from within the institution" could "strongly influence" the choices researchers made about "what problems they choose to tackle" (Stern 2016, 14). In particular, the REF was driving researchers towards "short-termism" and making them reluctant to tackle "risky or multidisciplinary projects", and more generally the REF "may be discouraging innovative thinking and risk-taking" (ibid.; see also Smith 2010). Even acknowledging the difficulty of collecting robust evidence of these unintended impacts of the REF process, Stern maintained that "there remains a concern" that the REF creates "distortions" in the ways that research happens in the UK (Stern 2016, 14). These distortions are one way in which policy – in this case, policy about measuring research quality and the distribution of research funding – shapes the research that can occur and consequently the evidence that might be available for policymaking.

Approach three: "co-production"

Given that both of the first two approaches that we have discussed are helpful for explaining some elements of HE policy, it seems sensible to combine them and suggest that evidence shapes policy *and* policy shapes evidence. It is not only that the REF restricts the kinds of research undertaken, but also that research undertaken in the UK (such as Smith 2010) influenced Stern's review of the REF and will lead to policy changes. It is not only that George Osborne looked at evidence gathered by UCAS when deciding to lift the cap on student numbers, but also that the expansion of the UK HE system might alter the kinds of research that are being conducted, as demand for particular disciplines shapes universities' priorities.

The field of science and technology studies (STS), and in particular the work of Sheila Jasanoff, takes this kind of approach further, arguing for a more fundamental connection between evidence and policy through "co-production" (Jasanoff 2004). She explains co-production as "shorthand" for the idea that "the ways in which we know and represent the world (both nature and society) are inseparable from the ways in which we choose to live in it" (ibid., 2). Under this approach, politics and policy shape knowledge and evidence, but "scientific and expert knowledge" is also part of the construction of politics and governance (Boswell and Smith 2017, 5). States both create and legitimise knowledge and are "made of knowledge", partly constituted by the kinds of knowledge and ways of knowing that are embedded in political processes (Jasanoff 2004, 3). The ways in which politics and policy are "made of knowledge" are varied, including the ways in which knowledge determines the kinds of problems and solutions that can be articulated, and the kinds of tools and technologies available to be "deployed in governing" (Pickering 1995, in: Boswell and Smith 2017, 5). This frames the connection between evidence and policy as something that is deeper and more complex than a simple addition of the first two approaches. Knowledge and politics produce each other and are produced together by that mutual relationship.

Policymakers' alma maters

This kind of co-productive relationship is difficult to identify, because it is necessarily embedded deeply in the ways in which we think and talk about politics and policy. However, we think that one place it can be spotted is in the link between policymakers' educational experiences and the kinds of policy that they choose to enact. One particularly vivid example of this is in the alma maters of the politicians holding the HE portfolio since the role of Minister of State for Universities was created in 2001. The five New Labour ministers who held the position from 2001 to 2010 had a wide range of university experiences. None of them studied the same subject, and they attended (or didn't attend) a wide variety of institutions: School of Oriental and African Studies (David Lammy); University of Wales, Cardiff (Bill Rammell); Hornsey College of Art and Cambridgeshire College of Arts and Technology (Kim Howells); London School of Economics and Political Science (Margaret Hodge); and leaving formal education at 15 (Alan Johnson). By contrast, of the five Conservative ministers who have held the role since 2010, four attended Oxford (David Willetts, Jo Johnson, Sam Gyimah and Chris Skidmore) and one Cambridge (Greg Clark). Two of them studied Modern History, two Politics, Philosophy and Economics, and one Economics.

These differing backgrounds seem to align quite closely with the key priorities of the New Labour, Coalition, and Conservative governments. For New Labour, a key focus was on widening access to HE by both aiming to increase participation to 50 per cent of the population and attempting to set up a fees and loans system that could support poorer students (Chitty 2014, 207–209). The Coalition and Conservative governments, by contrast, have reintroduced a focus on quality, standards, and excellence (Conservative Party 2015, 2017) while continuing to prioritise fairer access and increased participation. The divisions between the priorities of the different parties are not neat, and there are undoubtedly some contradictions between the stated aims of the parties and the implications of their policy decisions (Chitty 2014, 212–213). However, we do think that the focus of government has seemed to shift back to a vision of HE shaped by elite universities, as the ministers with responsibility for HE have been more likely to have attended one of those elite universities themselves, and these policies in turn make it more likely that future members of the political elite will continue to come from a few select institutions. This example illustrates the importance of understanding our own biases and how our experience and ideas about knowledge shape the kinds of policy that we are open to, and vice versa.

Approach four: "autonomous spheres"

The final approach to theorising the relationship between evidence and policy that we will discuss is completely different to the three discussed earlier. It argues that the production of knowledge happens in a totally separate space to the practice of policymaking. One influential version of this is what Nathan Caplan calls the "two communities" theory, which he identifies as the "most prevalent" explanation given by social scientists for why their research is not used by policymakers (Caplan 1979, 459). Under the "two communities" theory, researchers and policymakers "live in separate worlds": the researcher's world is all "pure" science and the pursuit of the truth; the policymaker's world is "action-oriented" and concerned with finding solutions to the most immediate problems (ibid.). The "gap" between these two communities is at the core of the underutilisation of research in policymaking. Caplan's gap can fundamentally be filled by links and collaboration, if the communities wish. A more extreme version of this approach comes from systems theory, and in particular the work of Niklas Luhmann (Luhmann 1995; Boswell and Smith 2017). Under this theory, science (including social science) and politics (including policymaking) are completely separate, self-referential systems that do not interact (Boswell and Smith 2017, 6). They each operate according to their own languages, codes, and logics, and any supposed interaction between the systems is actually an instance of parts of one system perceiving parts of another by giving them meaning through their own codes and logics.

Freedom of speech

The storm surrounding free speech within universities reflects how policy and evidence can talk at complete cross purposes, as if in different "systems". In October 2017, Jo Johnson, Universities Minister 2016–2018, directed England's newly created HE regulator, the Office for Students, to work with universities to create "a culture of openness and debate", citing "examples of censorship where groups have sought to stifle those who do not agree with them" (Department for Education 2017), this despite a 2016 survey commissioned by ChangeSU, which found that of the 50 students' unions surveyed, none had banned speakers in the previous year (ChangeSU 2016). In March 2018, the House of Commons and House of Lords Joint Committee on Human Rights published a report into freedom of speech in universities after "concerns expressed by Parliamentary colleagues, Ministers and the media that student attitudes were undermining free speech in universities" (House of Commons and House of Lords Joint Committee on Human Rights 2018, 4). The Committee stated that they "did not find the wholesale censorship of debate in universities which media coverage has suggested" (ibid., 20). Nevertheless, Sam Gyimah (who succeeded Johnson as Minister for Universities in 2018), continued to discuss freedom of speech in universities, insisting that "[t]his is a real problem and we've got to deal with it" (Busby 2018). Successive Universities Ministers have seemed to be talking at complete cross purposes with the evidence, sustained by a political environment (or "system") in which that evidence is irrelevant.

Conclusion

The first two approaches that we have discussed – "evidence shapes policy" and "policy shapes evidence" – each seem to capture something about the policymaking process. The idea that evidence shapes policy is at the very least the aspiration of many policymakers. The acknowledgement that policy shapes evidence does get at some truth about the influence of politics over research. However, neither of these is sufficient: the simplification of policymaking into a linear process (in either direction) fails to capture the complexity of the relationship between evidence and policy. This suggests that we need, at a minimum, to think about both the role that evidence plays in shaping policy and the role that policy plays in shaping evidence. Both the third and fourth approaches that we have outlined allow us to do this. Co-production provides a framework for thinking about the policy and evidence as mutually productive, shaping each other continuously. Caplan's "two communities" and Luhmann's systems theory provide a way of thinking about how or why policy and evidence play a minimal role in shaping one another.

We believe that the first of these more complex approaches – co-production – offers opportunities for a far more positive, productive relationship. We should be seeking to close the gap, to ensure that we are not speaking at cross purposes, that we are operating within one system. Acknowledging the role of co-production brings its own challenges: as researchers and policymakers we should be reflective, considering how the relationships we build, the evidence we look to and the policies we consider are constrained. Without this reflection, and deliberate effort, the likelihood of a disconnect increases. This in turn increases the likelihood of policy outcomes that are entirely separate from evidence, or of a system that reinforces itself within a small, self-referential bubble.

References

Bailey, LF and G Scott-Jones (1984) Rational, irrational and other reasons for commissioning research. *Marketing Intelligence & Planning*, 2(3), 36–50.

Boswell, C and K Smith (2017) Rethinking policy "impact": four models of research-policy relations. *Palgrave Communications*, 3(44), 1–10.

Busby, E (2018) Minister claims lecturer reported for "hate speech" teaching history, sparking angry denials. *The Independent*. Available from: www.independent.co.uk/news/education/education-news/free-speech-hate-crime-university-lecturers-students-kings-college-london-sam-gyimah-berlin-a8399081.html

Cabinet Office (1999) *Modernising Government*. London: The Stationery Office.

Cabinet Office (2013) *What Works*: Evidence Centres for Social Policy. London: Crown Copyright.

Caplan, N (1979) The two-communities theory and knowledge utilization. *American Behavioural Scientist*, 22(3), 459–470.

ChangeSU (2016) *Our Sector: Freedom of Speech and SUs – What's Really Going On?* Available from: www.changesu.org/?p=576

Chitty, C (2014) *Education Policy in Britain*, 3rd edn. London: Palgrave Macmillan.

Conservative Party (2015) *The Conservative Party Manifesto 2015.* London: Conservative Party. Available from: www.conservatives.com/manifesto2015

Conservative Party (2017) *The Conservative Party Manifesto 2017.* London: Conservative Party. Available from: www.conservatives.com/manifesto

Department for Education (2017) *Jo Johnson Calls for Free Speech to Be Protected on Campus.* London: Department for Education. Available from: www.gov.uk/government/news/jo-johnson-calls-for-free-speech-to-be-protected-on-campus

HC Deb (2013) vol. 571, col. 1107. London: House of Commons. Available from: https://publications.parliament.uk/pa/cm201314/cmhansrd/cm131205/debtext/131205-0002.htm

Hillman, N (2014) *A Guide to the Removal of Student Number Controls.* Oxford: Higher Education Policy Institute. Available from: www.hepi.ac.uk/wp-content/uploads/2014/09/Clean-copy-of-SNC-paper.pdf

House of Commons and House of Lords Joint Committee on Human Rights (2018) *Freedom of Speech in Universities: Fourth Report of Session 2017–2019.* Available from: publications.parliament.uk/pa/jt201719/jtselect/jtrights/589/589.pdf

Jasanoff, S (2004) The idiom of co-production. In: S Jassanoff, ed. *States of Knowledge: The Co-production of Science and the Social Order.* London: Routledge.

Luhmann, N (1995) *Social Systems.* Stanford, CA: Stanford University Press.

Naughton, M (2005) "Evidence-based policy" and the government of the criminal justice system – only if the evidence fits! *Critical Social Policy*, 25, 47–69.

Nutley, SM, I Walter, and HTO Davies (2007) *Using Evidence: How Research Can Inform Public Services.* Bristol: The Policy Press.

Policy Lab (2018) *About Policy Lab.* Available from: openpolicy.blog.gov.uk/about/

REF (2011) *Decisions on Assessing Research Impact.* Bristol: Hefce. Available from: ref.ac.uk/2014/pubs/2011-01/

REF (2017) *Initial Decisions on the Research Excellence Framework 2021 (REF 2017/01).* Bristol: Hefce. Available from: www.ref.ac.uk/publications/initial-decisions-on-the-research-excellence-framework-2021-ref-201701

Research England (n.d.) *How We Fund Research.* Swindon: UK Research and Innovation. Available at: https://re.ukri.org/research/how-we-fund-research/

Royal Society (2017) *Policy Projects Reforms to the UK's Higher Education, Research and Innovation System.* London: The Royal Society. Available from: royalsociety.org/topics-policy/projects/higher-education-research-innovation-system/

Sasse, T and S Haddon (2018) *How Government Can Work with Academia.* London: Institute for Government.

Smith, K (2010) Research, policy and funding – academic treadmills and the squeeze on intellectual spaces. *The British Journal of Sociology*, 61(1), 176–195.

Stern, N (2016) *Building on Success and Learning from Experience: An Independent Review of the Research Excellence Framework.* London: Crown Copyright.

Stevens, A (2007) Survival of the ideas that fit: an evolutionary analogy for the use of evidence in policy. *Social Policy and Society*, 6, 25–35.

Stevens, A (2011) Telling policy stories: an ethnographic study of the use of evidence in policy-making in the UK. *Journal of Social Policy*, 40(2), 237–255.

UCAS (2011) *Admissions Process Review Consultation.* Cheltenham: Universities and Colleges Admissions Service. Available from: www.ucas.com/file/956/download?token=y8EovXLo

Weiss, CH (1977) Research for policy's sake: the enlightenment function of social research. *Policy Analysis*, 3, 531–547.

Weiss, CH (1979) The many meanings of research utilization. *Public Administration Review*, 39(5), 426–431.

Westwood, A (2013, 5 December) A statement that we didn't expect? *Wonkhe.* Available from: wonkhe.com/blogs/a-statement-that-we-didnt-expect/

Wyatt, A (2002) Evidence based policy making: the view from a centre. *Public Policy and Administration*, 17(3), 12–28.

CHAPTER 4

Working with think-tanks

Diana Beech

Introduction

When it comes to influencing policy, the power of think-tanks is not to be underestimated. This is especially true in the field of higher education (HE), given its increasingly important role in the national policy agenda and its clear linkages to economic growth, global competitiveness, and social mobility. In this chapter, I provide an introduction to the role of think-tanks in influencing policy at the broadest level, before providing an in-depth look at how think-tanks operate in the UK HE space. Given my former role as the first Director of Policy and Advocacy at the Higher Education Policy Institute (HEPI) – the UK's only HE-specialist think-tank – I reflect extensively on HEPI's work and provide personal insights into what working for a think-tank entails. I also use my subsequent position as Policy Adviser to the Universities Minister to consider how think-tanks can help maximise their influence in government. I trust my experiences will prove useful, not only for those considering joining a think-tank at some point in their careers, but for anyone looking to harness the potential of think-tanks to enrich debate about HE and create better policy and processes for the future.

What is a think-tank?

The term "think-tank" made its debut in the *Oxford English Dictionary* in 1958 and is nowadays defined as a "research institute or other organization providing advice and ideas on national or commercial problems; an interdisciplinary group of specialist consultants" (OED Online n.d.). The term think-tank is nevertheless far from self-evident, and one would be forgiven for not understanding fully what it is that a think-tank does from its name alone. Those working in a think-tank do indeed spend their time "thinking" but to reduce their work purely to the generation of ideas does a gross disservice to the complexity of their wider operations.

It is by no coincidence that think-tanks share their name with heavily armoured military vehicles. Both require ammunition, both have targets, and both require a high degree of resilience. Whereas conventional tanks rely on weapons aimed at adversaries, think-tanks use the evidence they gather to promote healthy debate and target policy change at the highest levels of government. Strategically manoeuvring a think-tank requires much more than robust research and analysis, however. Troops need to be rallied through continuous advocacy and sector engagement, and supporters and allies must be forged through a comprehensive programme of development activities. These latter undertakings are essential for establishing and maintaining partnerships that will serve to generate new ideas and fund future work. In short, they are the power behind a think-tank's fire.

Think-tank staff work round the clock to shape policy by conducting research, disseminating results, and advocating for change. To be effective, think-tanks must be reactive and proactive in equal measure. This involves monitoring policy developments and responding to change, as well as looking ahead for fresh opportunities to influence debate with new ideas and momentum. Having a future plan of attack is, therefore, just as important for a think-tank's success as engaging with ongoing battles.

Types of think-tanks

Groups of thinkers coming together to influence political life have existed since the dawn of democracy. Yet, it was not until the late twentieth century that the modern think-tank, as we know it, came to prominence in the British political landscape, gaining particular influence in the Thatcher years and, again, under New Labour. (Cockett 1995). Think-tanks have since become a key part of the UK policymaking apparatus and continue to grow in number. New think-tanks are being established all the time as different ideas and influences emerge and individuals seek new ways to connect with those in power. As the late political commentator Anthony Howard once quipped: "It's rather like in medieval times when you would have set up a monastery. Now you set up a think-tank. It brings you into the swim of things" (Rohrer 2008).

While think-tanks in the UK may be numerous, they are certainly not homogenous. Think-tanks come in a variety of shapes and sizes, and can best be thought of in three distinct groups. The first group comprises broad-based or "generalist" think-tanks, some, but not all, of which are associated with a specific political agenda or cause. Prominent examples of generalist think-tanks include Policy Exchange and Reform, which research diverse policy issues across a wide range of sectors and industries. The second type of think-tanks can be referred to as "issue-driven" think-tanks, which promote thinking on a specific topic or theme that cuts across multiple policy areas. One example of an issue-driven think-tank is the Resolution Foundation, which works to improve living standards for those in Britain on low to middle incomes and thereby covers several policy areas including housing, welfare, employment, and education. Finally, the third group of think-tanks includes subject-specific or "specialist" think-tanks, which focus in on a single field or policy area – at either a macro- or a micro-specialist level. When it comes to looking at HE policy in the UK, the Education Policy Institute (EPI) covers HE at the macro-specialist level as part of its remit looking at early years through to post-18 education, while the Higher Education Policy Institute (HEPI) covers it at the micro-specialist level through its exclusive focus on HE.

Who works at a think-tank?

Anthony Seldon, co-editor of a two-volume book analysing the role of think-tanks in contemporary Britain (Kandiah and Seldon 1996/1997), previously expressed scepticism about the influence of think-tanks, claiming that true influence "comes from people who break off from them and come into government" (Rohrer 2008). As someone who moved on from a think-tank to work at the heart of government policymaking, I am not going to deny that think-tanks can be ideal training grounds for the next generation of politicians and advisers. However, I also believe that who goes on to work at a think-tank following a key policy role can be just as important to an organisation's status and influence as where people move on to afterwards. It is, after all, no coincidence that many of the most influential think-tanks in the UK are headed up by former civil servants, special advisers, party activists, journalists, or politicians – all of whom bring with them valuable institutional memory from within Westminster and Whitehall and know how politics works. This is essential for understanding both how to promote a think-tank's work and to whom to pitch it.

As well as relying on strong, experienced leadership, think-tanks also need a wealth of brain power. Working at a think-tank can be an attractive career move for fresh graduates, as well as established researchers, writers, and analysts – some of whom may be hoping for a springboard into future political careers. This high rate of personnel exchange between the think-tank world and the policy world is ultimately what helps to keep a think-tank at the top of its game, ensuring a constant influx of fresh ideas and talent, as well as a necessary outflow of key influencers who will remain loyal to a think-tank long after they have left.

How think-tanks are funded

The work of think-tanks is largely defined by their mission and source of funding. In an idealised world, think-tanks would be independent, dispassionate organisations working to effect outcomes that are genuinely best for the policy area in question. Yet, running a think-tank costs money and, without principled leadership or governance in place, some think-tanks may be tempted to sell their editorial line in return for financial contributions. In a society where money talks, some funders may choose to attach conditions to their gifts, with the result that recipient think-tanks end up being led by the whims and desires of those who bankroll them. Without a free rein to study whatever they choose, these think-tanks can quickly lose their impartiality and objectivity and may end up producing conclusions which unashamedly endorse their funder's products or philosophy. Such organisations are more akin to campaign or lobby groups.

The clue to a think-tank's independence (or otherwise) is in its status, which should be openly declared on its website and/or publications. Some think-tanks are registered as private companies or campaign groups, which allows them to pursue a particular political vision. Such think-tanks may choose to be politically aligned or remain non-partisan and independent. Many think-tanks have been established as charities, which means they must follow strict rules about political activity to comply with both charity law and public expectations. Think-tanks established as charities may not have a political purpose but are still free to get their funding in different ways – including through donations, sponsorship opportunities, membership fees or partnership programmes. Other think-tanks may choose to remain non-charitable or for-profit. This usually applies to think-tanks which are aligned to businesses, such as the research departments of major consulting firms (see the Economist Intelligence Unit, for example), which effectively serve to market their companies' wider products and services.

The best way to tell a genuinely independent think-tank from one which may be "compromised" is via its commitment to transparency. The most independent think-tanks will be forthcoming about their sources of income, and a good indicator of impartiality is if these sources are wide-ranging. It is, therefore, always worth checking a think-tank's website for details of its funding streams or looking at its publications for information on which external organisations may have supported its work. The "Who Funds You?" campaign, which promotes funding transparency among UK think-tanks, also provides ratings for the country's largest think-tanks based on how open they are about their sources of income and the amounts given. The think-tanks providing the most information about their funding are given the highest "Band A" rating, while those remaining opaque about their funding are given the lowest "Band E" rating.

Table 4.1 incorporates some of this data and illustrates how a selection of think-tanks operating in the field of UK HE policy can differ in their size, type, funding, and transparency, despite all being registered as charities. The table uses 2018 data from the Charity Commission website plus information from the organisations' own websites. It also includes details on the leadership of each organisation (correct at the time of writing) to reinforce the importance of previous experience in the policy world for running a successful think-tank.

Table 4.1 Think-tanks active in UK higher education policy

Think-tank	Type	Leadership	Declared funding sources	Income	Expenditure	Employees	Who Funds You? rating (if applicable)
Education Policy Institute (EPI)	Specialist (macro)	Executive Chairman: David Laws, former politician	Foundations, organisations or individual members and event partners	£1.2m	£1.1m	16	n/a
Higher Education Policy Institute (HEPI)	Specialist (micro)	Director: Nick Hillman, former special adviser	Partner organisations and universities	£538,200	£449,900	4	n/a
Policy Exchange	Generalist	Director: Dean Godson, former journalist and political biographer	Unclear	£3.6m	£3.8m	27	E
Reform	Generalist	Director: Charlotte Pickles, former expert advisor to Iain Duncan Smith	Individual donors and corporate partners	£912,900	£1.1m	16	C
Resolution Foundation	Issue-driven	Director: Torsten Bell, former Labour Party Director of Policy	Resolution Trust and partners	£1.6m	£1.4m	16	B

How to engage with think-tanks

Engaging with think-tanks can clearly be an effective way for individuals and organisations to reach influential audiences. For those wishing to work with think-tanks to explore a particular issue, the best way to start is to find a think-tank which operates in the policy area that interests you and aligns with your overall mission. You should then take the time to understand the implications of working with that think-tank. For example, if your chosen think-tank is politically aligned then you will have to consider whether you are comfortable risking appearing partisan. The next thing to consider is what you want out of the arrangement: if depth of engagement in a particular issue is the aim, then smaller, specialist think-tanks may offer unrivalled access to relevant networks and expertise. However, if a wider reach is the target, then working with larger, more generalist think-tanks may help to attract broader audiences – although not necessarily with the same depth of debate and discussion. Timing and resource considerations may also influence your decision. While larger think-tanks may appear to have more capacity to undertake work at short notice or to tight deadlines, they may well turn out to be more rigid when it comes to business planning and allocation of resources. Smaller think-tanks may, instead, be nimbler in their approach to assignments, and potentially more competitive on price.

The kind of relationship you want to have with a think-tank should always be negotiable. This may range from approaching a think-tank to do a one-off piece of consultancy work to establishing a long-lasting partnership through which a think-tank will regularly design projects, conduct research and disseminate outputs. Most think-tanks are open to direct approaches and contact details can be found on organisational websites. It is not uncommon for think-tanks established as charities to enquire about motives behind any new proposals to ensure they will not jeopardise their charitable objectives. It is also not unreasonable to be asked by a think-tank to cover the costs of any additional resource that may be required including, for example, the services of market research companies. For think-tanks with a genuine desire to influence policy for the better, these costs should not be extortionate. Genuine think-tanks should seek only to cover their basic outgoings, as they will always be more interested in creating sustained partnerships and earning respect, as opposed to making profit.

How think-tanks differ from academia

Despite conducting their own analysis, think-tanks are different from traditional academic research institutes. While it is not uncommon for academic research to conclude by recommending further study or investigation, research published by think-tanks should be solutions-focused, concluding with practical recommendations for consideration and implementation by appropriate stakeholders. This is because, unlike academia, think-tanks always start with the policy rather than the question. Another key difference between research published by think-tanks and academic research is its accessibility, style, and tone. In academia, the transmission of research is generally considered more important than its reception, as scholars publish papers or monographs principally to demonstrate a significant contribution to knowledge. Yet, it is widely accepted that these outputs will generally not be read by anyone outside the relevant field. Think-tanks, by contrast, produce work which is intended to be read and acted upon by "generalists" – including politicians, civil servants, journalists, and the public. This makes the reception of ideas for think-tanks just as important as their transmission.

To deliver maximum impact, a think-tank's outputs should always be written in simple, straightforward language, avoid the use of jargon and be direct in its "asks". This is particularly pertinent when it comes to influencing government, as busy officials are, by and large, not going to have the time to sit down and read through swathes of political theory, convoluted language, or complicated methodologies. This means think-tanks need to strike a balance between providing just enough detail to demonstrate credibility on the one hand, yet not providing too much so as to obscure their main message on the other. Think-tank staff should always strive to produce material that is short, "punchy", and to the point.

How think-tanks differ from communications outlets

Despite needing to appeal to wide audiences, think-tanks are not communications agencies. Although many think-tanks often respond to policy developments with statements or blogs, it is not the chief responsibility of a think-tank to provide instant comment on current affairs. The press and other media outlets exist for that. The pressure for think-tanks to engage "in real time" with policy developments has arguably increased over recent years with the advent of social media. However, a think-tank's work should always be firmly rooted in evidence, and providing comment on wide-ranging issues can run the risk that opinion and uninformed judgement take precedence. For a think-tank, the old adage "think before you speak" must always ring true, and a think-tank's time is always going to be better spent conducting detailed policy analysis before making considered, evidence-based recommendations. It is this approach which will help protect its credibility and expertise for the future.

Moreover, think-tanks must be careful not to be distracted by the lure of making front-page headlines. Of course, media coverage helps a think-tank's ideas to gain traction and get noticed by a wide range of stakeholders – not to mention attract future funders. However, securing a front-page splash must not always be the end game for a think-tank or, indeed, its ultimate measure of success. When it comes to judging how successful a think-tank is at influencing policy, much depends on its ability to reach the people who really count. In this respect, getting a paper out to a select group of senior leaders behind closed doors can be much more effective than securing a primetime slot on the six o'clock news – reinforcing the notion that for a think-tank the duty to consider the *quality* and not the *quantity* of an audience must always be paramount.

How think-tanks differ from lobby groups

Even though their outputs can be used as a tool for lobbyists, think-tanks are not lobby groups. While there is a growing responsibility on think-tanks to become more "activist" to reach those in positions of influence, their work must always be firmly guided by evidence. This means think-tanks can often appear inconsistent in their approach and may find themselves endorsing government policy in one area, yet arguing against government decisions in another. This is completely normal for an evidence-led organisation. Genuinely independent think-tanks, driven by interest in improving policy for the better, should always be unafraid to hold different stakeholders to account – be these individuals, organisations, the media, or local and national governments. They should not be forced to adopt institutional "lines", especially by those who fund them, and individuals within a think-tank should be free to hold different positions or opinions based on the evidence they collect. This is a sign of free and healthy debate. Independent think-tanks should never aim to endorse policies based on their politics (i.e. depending on whether they are right-wing or left-wing), but they should always seek to implement the "best" policy for the subject in question, irrespective of ideological origins. This is a far cry from lobby groups, which tend to represent causes or push for policies in line with specific political or ideological sympathies. As such, lobby groups' stances are not only largely predictable, but also often inflexible. Whereas lobby groups are generally bound only to tackle topics which their funders deem acceptable, genuinely independent think-tanks are free to be fleet of foot and take opportunities to influence debate without risk of alienating their core supporters or cutting off income streams.

How think-tanks exert influence

Think-tanks have a wealth of options to convey their messages to the outside world. The most traditional think-tanks produce written reports for publication either in hard copy or digital format (or both). These reports should be publicly available. If housed behind paywalls, questions need to be asked about the think-tank's mission and whether it is genuinely trying to effect meaningful policy change. The rise in popularity of social media in recent years has clearly allowed the reach of even the smallest organisation to expand exponentially, with reports on UK-only policy issues now being read and reacted to by people from across the world. This has helped to raise the profile of think-tanks' work, as well as widen the parameters of discussion to include international comparisons and contributions.

Producing reports is nevertheless only the start of a think-tank's programme of external engagement. Busy politicians and industry leaders are not necessarily going to be inclined to read a hefty report, so a comprehensive programme of communications and engagement is essential to ensure a think-tank's work reaches all its desired audiences. This can involve:

- giving media and press agencies advance sighting of research to ensure coverage in local and national press;
- repackaging findings and recommendations in shorter, easy-to-access formats such as blogs or op-eds;
- taking part in media interviews on TV, radio, or in print;
- using a range of social media platforms to promote awareness of work;
- hosting launch events for publications; or
- arranging strategic one-to-one meetings with key stakeholders.

In addition, it is not unusual for think-tank staff to get themselves on to the "speaking circuit" and take part in relevant sector events. This could involve giving keynote papers at conferences or taking part in panel discussions. For members of small think-tanks seeking to get themselves known to wider audiences, it can be tempting to accept all speaking opportunities that come their way. However, given how demanding think-tank life is, it is often wise to be selective and agree to only those activities that offer something tangible for the individual or organisation in return. Too many corporate organisations turn to think-tank staff to chair often over-priced, day-long events, without even offering so much as expenses as compensation. We have all fallen into this trap at some point in our think-tank lives, but sometimes the only effective way to learn what is worthwhile and what is not is through trial and error.

Where think-tanks seek to influence

The target audience for a think-tank varies depending on its remit, political association (if applicable), and policy area. Those seeking to promote healthy policy debate at the national level generally engage with individuals or institutions in their specific policy field, relevant sector bodies, and parliamentarians of all political colours at the national, local, and perhaps even international levels. To be effective, think-tanks do not always have to set their sights on influencing the highest echelons of government. Sometimes the most effective policy changes to be made are at the institutional level. Working with industry leaders can therefore be just as impactful and lead to positive outcomes.

For a think-tank seeking to influence HE policy in the UK, the stakeholder landscape is complex, and success can depend on effectively engaging with multiple individuals or organisations at any one time. These include (although are in no way restricted to):

- politicians (local, national, and international, as well as from the devolved administrations);
- HE providers;
- sector regulators;
- mission groups and representative bodies;
- student societies;
- academic and support staff;
- unions;
- research funders and charitable trusts;
- accommodation providers;
- academic publishers; and
- data and technology companies.

Depending on the policy area in question, think-tanks seeking to influence HE policy should be mindful about who they engage with within these organisations. Given the complexity of HE institutions, in particular, it may well be more advantageous to liaise with representatives from relevant departments or individual service providers, rather than go directly to senior leaders who may have less depth of understanding or influence over a technical issue.

How think-tanks fit into the higher education policy landscape

To the untrained eye, the HE policy world may already appear congested with different organisations, all vying to conduct research, host policy events, and provide media comment. Many of these organisations are mission groups (e.g. University Alliance, MillionPlus, or the Russell Group) or representative bodies (Universities UK, GuildHE) – each seeking to speak up for different parts of the HE sector with similar origins, values, and ambitions. None of these organisations is either truly independent or impartial. Many are membership organisations and, as such, have an explicit duty to look out for the best interests of their subscribers. The outputs they produce will inevitably paint their members in a positive light and the policy change they campaign for will largely be directed at national government, external authorities, or even other parts of the sector. Similarly, the trade press in HE may unfailingly champion the sector: its readership depends on it. No sensible editor is ever going to alienate readers by playing host to voices which are overwhelmingly critical of the sector's value or position. Articles hosted by these outlets are largely produced *by* the sector *for* the sector and, as such, run the risk of becoming echo chambers or, at the very least, rallying grounds for the benefits of HE. What this means from the policy-maker's perspective, then, is that the evidence governments receive to support policy change is nearly always put together by those with a vested interest in protecting their corner of the market. Separating out the trustworthy sources from the clearly biased ones can be a difficult task.

This is where think-tanks can come in. Unlike mission groups, representative bodies, or sector press, think-tanks are able to give space to a wide variety of views about the sector – from its failings to its successes, and from its critics to its supporters. Think-tanks operating in HE can fill the void that has emerged between government, universities, the public, and the press and hold a much-needed mirror up to a sector which spends its time analysing processes and procedures in industries other than its own. By acting as an "honest broker" in a field of competing views about the value and purpose of HE, a think-tank can test ideas on neutral ground and make recommendations to various stakeholders without fear of losing income or support. It is in this way that a think-tank can quickly become a respected go-to source of knowledge and evidence for universities and government alike.

The role of the Higher Education Policy Institute

As the UK's only independent think-tank exclusively devoted to HE, it is useful to look at the Higher Education Policy Institute (HEPI) to gain a better idea of how a specialist think-tank operates in the HE space and helps to promote healthy policy debate; HEPI is a rarity in the think-tank world in that it is not headquartered in London. HEPI was established in Oxford in 2002 by Bahram Bekhradnia – former Director of Policy at the now defunct Higher Education Funding Council for England (Hefce). Bekhradnia founded HEPI out of a concern about the lack of impartial evidence to shape HE policy. He was succeeded as director in 2013 by Nick Hillman, who was previously the Special Adviser to the Minister for Universities and Science, the Rt Hon (now Lord) David Willetts. HEPI's strong links with the policy world are therefore clear for all to see and have helped the think-tank to build effective bridges between the HE sector on the one hand and the world of Whitehall and Westminster on the other.

HEPI's remit is national, covering the four UK HE systems. It is non-partisan and is a registered charity, as well as a company limited by guarantee.

HEPI aims to be as transparent as possible about both its funding and its spending. It was originally funded by Hefce but became self-reliant by establishing two parallel partnership programmes – one for HE institutions and another for businesses that wish to see a healthy and vibrant UK HE sector. Partner organisations have the opportunity to influence HEPI's agenda by providing ideas for publications and events; however, they do not have a say over any conclusions or recommendations arising from HEPI's work. HEPI influences HE policy in three key ways: by producing topical policy reports, by contributing to public debates and by hosting a wide range of events (from which it also receives additional income). To date, HEPI has produced around 150 publications which are all available freely online. HEPI reports come in a variety of formats. Its flagship annual report – the *Student Academic Experience Survey* – has historically been produced in partnership with the Higher Education Academy (since merged into Advance HE) and is highly cited within the sector. It has been used to track trends such as students' perceptions of value for money for HE. As its profile has grown, the survey has become an essential source of information for government, having been referred to by the former Universities Minister, Jo Johnson, and endorsed by the Office for Students (Johnson 2017; Office for Students 2018).

The *Student Academic Experience Survey* is, however, just one of many reports HEPI produces in conjunction with partners. Other examples include a 2017 report produced with Unite Students, an accommodation provider – *Reality Check: A Report on University Applicants' Attitudes and Perceptions* – and a 2018 report produced in partnership with Kaplan International Pathways, an HE provider, and London Economics, a specialist consultancy – *The Costs and Benefits of International Students by Parliamentary Constituency*. Despite its strong collaborative approach, HEPI's editorial independence is keenly guarded by an advisory board and trustees, who conduct a rigorous peer-review process on all its major projects prior to publication. HEPI's advisory board meets three times a year and accepted papers are traditionally published within the four months leading up to the next advisory board meeting. This means publishing work through HEPI offers authors far quicker turnaround times than academic journals, as well as other advantages including promotional activities at the time of publication (through HEPI's blog and growing social media presence) and guaranteed longevity through HEPI's online repository.

With the exception of its one-off reports, the vast majority of HEPI reports are instantly recognisable for their small "blue book" format – none of which is more than 10,000 words in length and must adhere to a strict style guide to ensure simplicity as well as quality. Alongside these blue books, HEPI also publishes an "occasional paper" series. These are usually informed polemical pieces from people with long experience working in the HE sector. HEPI reports generally receive strong media coverage in local, national, and sector press, and the organisation is regularly called on to provide comment across a wide range of HE issues on TV, radio, and in print. Its staff also take part in prominent sector events and frequently address HEPI's partners on request to provide sector updates or talks on key policy developments. In addition, the think-tank maintains a busy events programme of its own, with the two most significant events in the HEPI calendar being its annual conference (summer) and annual lecture (winter).

The future for think-tanks in higher education

As HEPI's sustained success demonstrates, there is a clear demand for a specialist HE think-tank in the UK – one which can continue to track students' views as a trusted third party, hold the sector and other stakeholders equally to account, and advocate for positive change. As developments in HE policy continue at pace, the demand for such an organisation is only underscored. New policy options will need to be invented, challenged, and debated in a safe yet stimulating environment. Moreover, as more and more stakeholders enter the frame – as technology progresses and the sector expands – a specialist think-tank can provide a neutral focal point where issues can be raised, responsibility shared, and problems resolved. This is particularly appealing to new HE providers, which may fall outside traditional mission group alignments and otherwise struggle to air their concerns. A specialist HE think-tank should always treat all stakeholders equally and thereby help dispel entrenched hierarchies in the sector and the dominance of certain institutions in influencing the policy agenda. A specialist think-tank should always strive to ensure policy works for the *whole* sector, meaning students, institutions, and politicians alike can rest assured its proposals are balanced to the needs of individuals, the sector, and the nation as a whole.

In a world where the costs of a university education are high – be it to individuals, the government, or wider society – the pressure to "get it right" when it comes to policy formation and implementation is only mounting. A specialist HE think-tank can, therefore, provide a helping hand to everyone involved and steer discussions in the right direction. To imagine the UK HE sector without a dedicated think-tank in the future is to deprive it of an invaluable and impartial critical friend.

References

Cockett, R (1995) *Thinking the Unthinkable: Think-Tanks and the Economic Counter-Revolution, 1931–83.* London: HarperCollins.

Johnson, J (2017, 20 July) *Delivering Value for Money for Students and Taxpayers.* Available from: www.gov.uk/government/speeches/jo-johnson-delivering-value-for-money-for-students-and-taxpayers

Kandiah, MD and A Seldon (1996/1997) *Ideas and Think-Tanks in Contemporary Britain*, Volumes 1 and 2. London: Routledge.

OED Online (n.d.). S.V. Oxford: Oxford University Press.

Office for Students (2018, 7 July) *Office for Students Responds to the 2018 HEPI Student Academic Experience Survey*. Available from: www.officeforstudents. org.uk/news-blog-and-events/press-and-media/office-for-students-responds-to-the-2018-hepi-student-academic-experience-survey/

Rohrer, F (2008, 15 January) Just what is a think-tank? *BBC News*. Available from: news.bbc.co.uk/1/hi/magazine/7189094.stm

CHAPTER 5

International organisations in higher education policymaking

The role of the OECD

Claire Randerson

Introduction

A complex network of both national and international education policy actors has emerged over recent decades. In an increasingly globalised field, understanding the role and significance of international organisations for a fuller understanding of education policymaking is crucial. A growing literature points to the role of international organisations in sharing best practices, showcasing innovative policies, agreeing common definitions and frameworks, and driving policy convergence and alignment of agendas in national and international settings. For education policy researchers and practitioners focused on the "developing" world, international organisations such as the World Bank and the United Nations Educational, Scientific and Cultural Organization (UNESCO) are influential policy actors addressing educational issues as part of broader development and poverty eradication agendas, while within the "developed" world, the Organisation for Economic Cooperation and Development (OECD) has become a central actor in new educational governance (Rizvi and Lingard 2010, 127).

Most research exploring the influence of international policy actors has thus far been directed towards the compulsory education sector, as opposed to the more specific area of higher education (HE). Where HE is the focus, the influence of the European Union and the Bologna Process/European Higher Education Area (EHEA) on national and institutional policy has tended to receive most attention. However, in the globalised field of education policy, the OECD has gradually emerged as an international actor of rising importance, an often-cited "eminence grise" (Rinne, Kallo, and Hokka 2004, 456; Martens and Jakobi 2009, 99) within education policy. As a prolific and credible publisher in this field and a source of extensive and valued comparative data, the OECD possesses influential tools capable of disseminating ideas, interrogating national HE systems and influencing education policy within countries.

The OECD

The origins of the OECD lie in the reconstruction of Europe's economy after World War Two and the Organisation for European Economic Co-operation (OEEC), created to administer Marshall Plan funding. Rooted in dominant liberal beliefs about the centrality of interdependence and cooperation as vital to the construction of a successful post-war new international economic order, the organisation reconstituted itself as the OECD in 1961, with an expanded membership to include the USA and Canada.

Today, the OECD's website proclaims a mission "to promote policies that will improve the economic and social well-being of people around the world", describing itself as providing "a forum in which governments can work together to share experiences and seek solutions to common problems" (OECD n.d. a). Variously depicted in the scholarly literature as a "global think tank", a "policy making forum", a "Rich man's club" (see Henry, Lingard, Rizvi, and Taylor 2001, 7) its membership has expanded beyond the original 20 Western countries to a (slightly) more geographically and culturally diverse grouping of 36, which together account for 80 per cent of world trade and investment (OECD n.d. b), and the organisation continues to expand. Membership of the OECD is open to countries committed to a market economy, liberal democracy, and respect for human rights. Taken together, these conditions create a more ideologically homogenous grouping than global organisations such as UNESCO, and while clear distinctions can be noted between European and Anglo-Saxon conceptualisations of markets and the role of the state (Henry et al. 2001, 8), this relative homogeneity facilitates the construction of consensus. The OECD's core structure consists of directorates, committees, and special bodies headed by the OECD Council of representatives comprising member countries and the European Commission (a non-voting participant since 1961). Council decisions are taken via consensus.

OECD and higher education

The OECD's involvement in education dates back to the very beginnings of the organisation; however, over time, the organisation's involvement in education has expanded significantly, becoming increasingly central to the OECD's core activities in economic development. Human capital theory, with its approach to education as an investment for the purposes of economic growth and societal cohesion, swiftly became the legitimating principle around which the organisation formulated its education policy advice (Papadopoulos 1994; Henry et al. 2001; Schuller and Vincent-Lancrin 2009; van der Wende 20011).

An organisationally distinct area of activity for education was created via the establishment of the Centre for Educational Research and Innovation

(CERI) in 1968 and the Education Committee in 1970. Initially education fell under the remit of a range of different directorates until the creation of a new Directorate for Education (2002) – now Education and Skills – the establishment of which was marked by the organisation's then Secretary General, Donald Johnstone, pronouncing, "education is a priority for OECD Member countries, and the OECD is playing an increasingly important role in this field. Society's most important investment is in the education of its people" (cited in Rizvi and Lingard 2010, 131). The establishment of a separate directorate for education is indicative of the growth in both stature and organisational priorities afforded to education policy in recent decades (Schuller and Vincent-Lancrin 2009). At the time of writing, headed by Andreas Schleicher, the Directorate for Education and Skills oversees a range of activities in its ambition to help member countries "strengthen social and economic participation through developing the right skills, and to improve the effectiveness and efficiency of institutions to make reform happen" (OECD 2018a, 82). Significant growth in the OECD's educational statistics production, and accompanying research and technical expertise, has helped provide the basis from which the organisation has built its ability to shape, coordinate, and converge education policy amongst member countries – a "policy entrepreneur" in the field of education (Martens and Jakobi 2009).

Both inside and outside the Directorate, the number of activities encompassing HE has increased since the mid-1990s. The organisation's interest in HE has emerged alongside the phenomenon of globalisation and a global convergence around neoliberal values. As a result, Rizvi and Lingard suggest that the values of democracy and equality within education policy discourse have been "rearticulated, subordinated to dominant economic concerns" (2010, 72), replaced by a dominant discourse around "imperatives of the global economy" (ibid. 79). As a response to globalisation, the OECD has encouraged the internationalisation of HE and in so doing has sought to establish for itself a specific policy coordination, research, and advocacy role that individual countries are arguably ill-equipped to undertake themselves. Within the OECD, the approach to education policy is framed by human capital theory and a view of HE as investment in both individual and national competitiveness within a global economy, hence "the private rate of return to graduates and the impact on productivity are key higher education indicators for the OECD" (Schuller and Vincent-Lancrin 2009, 68).

Tools of influence

While the OECD's role and influence have expanded into an area previously the exclusive competence of national governments, it has done so without the formal authority and implementation tools conventionally available to governments to ensure compliance. Equally, the OECD does not possess legal instruments in the area of education that require member countries to implement its decisions (Marcussen 2001; Martens, Balzer, Sackmann, and Wexmann 2004). As such, exploring the means via which the OECD exercises this influence, and is able to shape international and national education policy, is a crucial part of understanding the policy process.

To fulfil its purpose of influencing national policy and agendas in education, the OECD makes use of soft law and governance tools as "mechanisms of persuasion" (Henry et al. 2001, 2). As an organisation, it lacks the harder, resource-based, or regulatory power of other international actors such as the World Bank or the European Union, with their ability to proffer – or withhold – financial incentives and to regulate or legislate activities. Instead soft power tools are deployed in pursuit of its policy objectives (Schuller and Vincent-Lancrin 2009; Amaral and Neave 2009; Martens and Jackobi 2009). However, the influence of soft power instruments should not be underestimated. "Soft law is valuable on its own, not just as a stepping-stone to hard law. Soft law ... helps create normative 'covenants' and discourses that can reshape international politics" (Abbott and Snidal 2000, 456). Martens and Jacobi (2009) provide a valuable tripartite framework for analysing the governance tools deployed by the OECD, categorising them as "Agenda Setting", "Policy Formulation", and "Policy Coordination". Their research highlights the significance of these governance tools in relation to the OECD's successful dissemination of the paradigm of lifelong learning, now ubiquitous in the lexicon of education, but these tools are evident throughout OECD activities in the field of education.

Agenda-setting is a well-recognised facet of power (see Lukes 1974; Bachrach and Baratz 1962) and involves the ability to shape which issues are discussed and the parameters of these debates. In its role as think-tank, the OECD possesses significant discursive power to frame and conceptualize topics for policymakers, to shape conversations and agendas within HE (Henry et al. 2001; Martens and Jakobi 2009; van der Wende 2011) with CERI playing a notable role in this area. The OECD's discursive influence can be seen in works such as *Four Future Scenarios for Higher Education* (OECD 2006a) and *Higher Education to 2030* Volumes I and II (OECD 2008a; 2009). The former conceptualised a range of scenarios for HE depending on the varying extent of influence exerted by the variables of globalisation and government coordination. *Higher Education to 2030* is a foresight project (Schuller and Vincent-Lancrin 2009, 65), developing future scenarios focused around the areas of demography and globalisation with a view to structuring debate and influencing HE policy. Another facet of agenda-setting lies in the OECD's role of "ideational arbiter" (Marcussen 2001, 3), socialising the organisation's personnel, network of researchers, experts, and national civil servants into the values and mindset of the organisation. These individuals, often moving between international and national forums, then play their role in shaping opinions domestically (Amaral and Neave 2009).

Governance by Policy Formulation and Policy Coordination (Martens and Jacobi 2009) moves beyond agenda-setting to the production of policy recommendations, thereby seeking to shape directly the direction of policy inside countries and exercise a harmonising effect on members' policies. This takes place by means of the establishment of common standards/guidelines but also via the OECD's impressive data collection, data production, and data analysis capabilities, disseminated via its extensive publication outputs and conferences. These tools of influence will be explored in more detail later.

Recommendations and guidelines

The OECD has maintained an interest in internationalisation of HE since the early 1990s and the publication of *Internationalization of Higher Education* (OECD 1996b). Initially internationalisation was framed as increasing opportunities for international student mobility (van der Wende 2011, 96). However, by the turn of the millennium, market rationales for internationalisation had gained ground over political, social, or cultural motivations, positioning internationalisation in HE as a vital revenue-generating export industry. The use of trade as a lens via which to explore an educational activity or process was aided by the inclusion of trade in educational services as part of the World Trade Organisation's (WTO) GATS process for the first time (ibid., 97). CERI was mandated to explore internationalisation and trade in HE from 2002 and, as part of this process, an expert group was formed to develop a conceptual framework and to analyse emerging trends. The final report *Internationalisation and Trade in Higher Education* (OECD 2004a) highlighted new forms of educational mobility (programme, institutional, and professional – accompanying the more conventionally understood student mobility) and mapped these developments both geographically and by type of institutions, while highlighting the continuing importance of physical learning spaces – as opposed to e-learning (Schuller and Vincent-Lancrin 2009; van der Wende 2011). Jane Knight's influential and extensively cited framework of cross-border mobility emerged from this project (Schuller and Vincent-Lancrin 2009, 72) and the importance of trade in HE services for national economies resonates throughout the UK's *International Education Strategy: Global Growth and Prosperity* (BIS 2013).

In 2004, CERI published *Quality Assurance and Recognition in Higher Education: The Cross-Border Challenge* (OECD 2004b). This publication explored the challenges posed for national quality assurance procedures by cross-border education provision, in conjunction with issues related to professional mobility and recognition of qualifications, considering how member countries were responding to these particular challenges. Concluding that cross-border educational provision generally lay outside national quality assurance mechanisms, CERI's research raised concerns about leaving "students and other stakeholders vulnerable to low quality provision of cross border higher education" (ibid., 10) and highlighted both the need for, and challenges associated with, professional recognition of qualifications. Identifying a need for better regulatory frameworks, the OECD and UNESCO collaborated in the production of the 2005 *Guidelines in Quality Provision of Cross-border Higher Education* which, while non-binding in nature, call upon governments, institutions, and other stakeholders to develop quality-assurance frameworks to ensure the quality of cross-border educational services, to help students make informed choices and protect them from poor-quality provision, and work towards the international recognition, transparency, and portability of qualifications (OECD 2005). For Schuller and Lancrin, the guidelines "can be read as an educational response to globalization but also as a facilitator of trade" (2009, 79). This message was reinforced by the 2006 OECD ministerial conference in Athens which, under the new Secretary General, José Ángel Gurría, focused for the first time on HE in a conference which shifted policy emphasis from quantity (the size of HE systems), to the quality of HE systems (Schuller and Vincent-Lancrin 2009, 68; van der Wende 2011, 104).

Reviews: thematic and country

The OECD has undertaken thematic reviews of HE. The first of these, the 1996 *Thematic Review of Tertiary Education* (OECD 1996a) introduced the term "tertiary education" to the language of HE (van der Wende 2011, 104), while a second, the 2008 two-volume *Tertiary Education for the Knowledge Society* (OECD 2008b), is described by van der Wende as "probably the most comprehensive analysis ever taken in higher education" (2011, 105). This second review highlighted the importance of HE for raising skills in the context of an increasingly globalised economy and emphasised the need to improve educational quality and participation rates, alongside increasing the efficiency and accountability of HE institutions' governance. The review also encouraged institutions to develop and align their strategic priorities with those of their nation-state in meeting the challenges associated with globalisation (ibid.).

In addition to thematic reviews, the OECD also conducts country reviews to provide targeted analysis and advice for member countries, to share best practice, and to customise reports. For example, recent OECD reports have highlighted a need to address skill levels in the UK. A 2016 Country Report highlighted concerns that one in ten students in English HE had low basic skills (OECD 2016, 49) and in the 2017 OECD *Skills and Global Value Chains* report, the UK scored lower than many OECD member countries in cognitive skills and readiness to learn. The report gave specific policy advice for the UK to build graduate skills to ensure graduates were equipped "with strong mixes of relevant skills and reliable qualifications" (OECD 2017a, 2). The OECD's attention to graduate skills provides both valuable context for, and has contributed to, the ongoing search within the UK (and globally) for useable metrics to compare teaching quality, learning outcomes, and employability across HEIs and to measure students' learning gain.

Data collection, production, and analysis

The capacity of the OECD to collect and analyse data, to categorise and disseminate information, is a key dimension of the OECD's activities in the area of education, giving the organisation "extensive control of information on education" (Rinne et al. 2004, 456). The OECD's Indicator programme is central to its collection and production of education data. CERI developed the Indicators of Education Systems programme (INES) in 1988, a project which has since firmly established the OECD's influence in education. Shifting away from a reliance on nationally generated and often erroneous and unreliable data on educational inputs, towards a focus instead on outcome indicators (Martens and Jakobi 2009), INES provides "useful" statistics via which policymakers can evaluate and make cross-country comparisons of the effectiveness of national education systems, alongside generating data with which the OECD can promote best practice by particular countries. Mora and Felix assert that "most of the quantitative information that European higher education systems have used in the past five years comes from the annual publication *Education at a Glance*" (2009, 195). Introduced in 1991, this publication provides national and comparative data on education systems which includes HE data such as participation and completion levels, socio-economic indicators, labour market participation, minimum entry qualifications, and international student mobility – data "with direct relevance for the role of higher education as an investment in and producer of human capital in the context of global competition" (van Der Wende 2011, 103).

The OECD's Programme for International Student Assessment (PISA) is a triennial measurement of educational performance and outcomes of 15-year-olds in participating countries and is widely regarded as having been fundamental to the OECD's increasing influence in the area of education more broadly. PISA introduced standardised survey methods which facilitate cross-country comparisons and establish benchmarks which identify and promote examples of best practice (OECD n.d. c). The most recent PISA survey (2018) tested 15-year-olds from 79 states/economies, indicating the expanding geographic breadth of the OECD's influence. At the same time PISA 2018 broadened its testing from the usual academic subjects of mathematics, science and literacy to include "global competencies", pointing to a role for schools in ensuring that young people "not only learn to participate in a more interconnected world but also appreciate and benefit from cultural differences" and develop a "global and intercultural outlook" in order to live and work successfully in multicultural societies (OECD 2018b, 4). While only 28 countries have opted to test student skills in the global competence component of PISA (and only Scotland within the UK), it will be interesting to observe the future trajectory of this aspect of OECD work. The success and growth of PISA have bolstered the OECD's reputation as the leading provider of international education statistics and encouraged a widening of its gaze to include HE in the form of the OECD project Assessment of Higher Education Learning Outcomes (AHELO).

Regarded by some within the HE sector as a "PISA for higher education" (Olds 2010), the OECD sought to "carve a niche for itself to influence global policy in higher education" via the AHELO project, presented as "the first international study of what students in higher education know and can do upon graduation" (OECD 2012a, 2). Justified as an essential means of filling the gaps in comparative data on measuring the quality of teaching and student learning gain in HE globally and as a means of resolving quality assurance problems (Shahjahan and Torres 2013, 611), the AHELO feasibility study took place between 2010 and 2012, with the main study due to start in 2015. However, faced with complex metrics, resistance from "elite" institutions, and lack of enthusiasm from key member counties, the project was shelved in 2015 (Morgan 2015).

Despite this, the OECD's enthusiasm for comparative evaluation of HE systems has not ended with AHELO. More broadly, work on *Enhancing Higher Education System Performance* (OECD 2018c) and *Benchmarking Higher Education System Performance* (OECD 2017b) build on the OECD's previous experience in comparative statistical indicators, now applied to HE, to find out "what works" in terms of the performance of various HE sectors. Countries are therefore implicitly encouraged to ensure the efficiency and success of their own education systems by engaging in policy borrowing from "best practice" countries.

Policy analysis

The OECD also publishes analysis of its statistical data, formerly in the annual *Education Policy Analysis*, which in 2006 focused for the first time on HE (OECD 2006b), and more recently in *Education Policy Outlook*, which offers comparative analysis of reforms and trends in education policy

(OECD 2018d) and is specifically targeted at "policy makers, analysts and practitioners who seek information and analysis of education policy taking into account the national context" (OECD 2015, 2). The OECD's influence and reputation in the field of education policy have soared, both inside and outside the organisation, and inside states themselves: "its educational statistics and its review analyses are increasingly referred to by national policy makers as points of reference for national reform processes" (Martens et al. 2004, 4). For example, the 2015 *Education Policy Outlook* highlighted that a key challenge for the UK was to "improve student performance and reduce performance gaps between students of different socio-economic backgrounds" (OECD 2015, 4), contributing to the agendas of widening participation and learning gain within UK HE.

Similarly, in 2012 the Institutional Management of Higher Education (IMHE) project, *Approaches to Internationalisation and Their Implications for Strategic Management and Institutional Practice* (OECD 2012b), explored factors influencing internationalisation and approaches to managing internationalisation. Intended to enhance the ability of institutions and national governments to address the challenges of globalisation, the project encouraged institutions to internationalise for the benefit of students, research, and institutional profile. The project explored the relationship between national governments and HE institutions with a view to improving their approach to internationalisation and recommended a range of actions for both governments and institutions in their efforts to promote and managing internationalisation more effectively. Since this time, the UK government has published an international education strategy, emphasising international education as a revenue-generating form of global trade alongside briefly highlighting "the value of outward mobility for [the] employability" of UK-domiciled students (BIS 2013, 54), and the UK Higher Education International Unit (IU) produced the *UK Strategy for Outward Mobility 2013–2017*, the first UK-wide strategy promoting the outward mobility of UK-domiciled university students, followed by the successor strategy for 2017–2020 (UK Higher Education International Unit 2013; UUKi 2017).

Conclusion

Observing the OECD's activities in the field of education suggests a *deepening* – an increased intensity of policy activity – concurrent with a *broadening* of interest to encompass the increasingly distinct area of HE. Increased OECD activity in HE, and the internationalisation of HE more specifically, is viewed by a number of scholars as part of the organisation's response to globalisation (Rizvi and Lingard 2010; Amaral and Neave 2009), a phenomenon which has "transformed the discursive terms" (Rizvi and Lingard 2010, 117) underpinning debates around education policy and educational governance in which states have ceded some of their power and authority to international organisations. While is it clear that education policy remains largely a national exercise, it is equally apparent that above the level of the state exists a "magistrature of influence" (ibid., 123) emanating from international organisations via the establishment of standards and performance measures, in what Mundy (2007, 348) refers to as "standard setting multilateralism". Within this new form of governance, organisations such as the OECD encourage states in this transfer of power and authority as a means of addressing the fast-moving pace of change and the requirements of transnational organisations in a globalised world (Rizvi and Lingard 2010).

Despite the apparent weakness of the OECD's governance instruments, its tools of persuasion and influence have together raised the profile of the OECD's role in education. The OECD thus provides a forum for national comparison which facilitates policy transfer across state boundaries (Henry et al. 2001, 56), positioning the OECD as a "powerful agent in the convergence of national policies for higher education" (Amaral and Neave 2009, 95) and supporting the assertion that, not uncontroversially, "the OECD today not only defines the problem, it also offers the solution" (Martens and Jakobi 2009, 109). As such, the growing influence of the OECD in the field of education policy, its ability to shape policy and generate consensus, combined with its narrow focus on a marketisation model of education to the exclusion of other approaches, is the cause of disquiet amongst some scholars. The capacity of the OECD to collect and analyse data, to categorise and disseminate information, gives the organisation "extensive control of information on education" (Rinne et al. 2004, 456), raising legitimate questions about how policy agendas, examples of best practice, and innovation are identified and legitimised. Amaral and Neave express concern about the OECD's contribution to extending the "operational boundaries of neoliberalism" (2009, 95), with the associated positioning of education as "a private good and national economic good" (Rizvi and Lingard 2011, 20) and handmaid to the global economy.

Undoubtedly, more research is needed to explore the response of UK HE to the policy influence of the OECD, addressing how – or to what extent – recommendations emanating from the OECD find their way into national and institutional policy within HE. Equally, the ability of member countries to use organisations like the OECD to drive their own agenda remains relatively unexplored. Carroll (2010) explores the role and impact of the OECD within the country-specific setting of the Republic of Ireland's HE sector. He highlights the OECD's use of soft power instruments to transmit policies but suggests that soft power is exercised in both directions, from OECD policies and events but also from inside the member country, via the citation of OECD reports and analysis to "confer legitimacy" on key strategies and policies.

More broadly, growing interest in the role of international organisations, such as the OECD, is evident, and necessary. Scholarly work highlights a convergence of priorities and alignment of agendas across national and international structures and the OECD's sharing of best practice, showcasing of innovative policies, its testing and measurement tools, the establishment of common definitions and frameworks, drive this convergence. Although the extent, evenness, and the overall significance of this post-Westphalian politics are undeniably contestable, the importance of looking beyond the state for a fuller understanding of education policy influences and priorities is clear.

References

Abbott, KW and D Snidal (2000) Hard and soft law in international governance. *International Organization*, 45(3), 421–456.

Amaral, A and G Neave (2009) The OECD and its influence in higher education. In: RM Bassett and A Maldonado-Maldonado, eds. *International Organizations and Higher Education Policy: Thinking Globally, Acting Locally?* New York: Routledge.

Bachrach, P and MS Baratz (1962) Two faces of power. *The American Political Science Review*, 56(4), 947–952.

BIS (2013) *International Education: Global Growth and Prosperity.* London: Department for Business, Innovation and Skills. Available from: www.gov.uk/government/uploads/system/uploads/attachment_data/file/340600/bis-13-1081-international-education-global-growth-and-prosperity-revised.pdf

Carroll, P (2010) The OECD in Irish Higher Education: A Study of Two Policy Reviews. Doctor of Education thesis, Department of Education Studies, University of Sheffield. Available from: etheses.whiterose.ac.uk/14549/1/531238.pdf

Henry, M, B Lingard, F Rizvi, and S Taylor (2001) *The OECD, Globalisation and Education Policy.* Oxford: IAU Press and Pergamon, Elsevier Science.

Lukes, S (1974) *Power: A Radical View.* London: Macmillan.

Marcussen, M (2001) *The OECD in Search of a Role: Playing the Idea Game.* Prepared for presentation at the European Consortium for Political Research (ECPR), 29th Joint Sessions of Workshops, Grenoble, France, 6–11 April 2001. Available from: ecpr.eu/Filestore/PaperProposal/8472af10-56df-4518-87c2-7a35031ae678.pdf

Martens, K, C Balzer, R Sackmann, and A Wexmann (2004) Comparing governance of international organisations: the EU, the OECD and educational policy. TranState Working Papers Number 7. Available from: www.econstor.eu/bitstream/10419/28257/1/497810247.PDF

Martens K and AP Jakobi (2009) International organisations as governance actors: the OECD. In: I Dingeldey and H Rothgang, eds. *Education Policy in the Governance of Welfare State Reform: A Cross National and Cross Sectoral Comparison of Policy and Politics.* Cheltenham: Edward Elgar, pp. 94–112.

Mora, JG and J Felix (2009) European multinational regimes and higher education policy. In: RM Bassett and A Maldonado-Maldonado, eds. *International*

Organizations and Higher Education Policy: Thinking Globally, Acting Locally?
    New York: Routledge.
Morgan, J (2015, 21 September) OECD's AHELO will fail to launch, says education
    director. *Times Higher Education.* Available from: www.timeshighereducation.
    com/news/oecds-ahelo-will-fail-launch-says-education-director
Mundy, K (2007) Global governance, educational change. *Comparative Education,*
    43(3), 339–357.
OECD (n.d. a) *About the OECD.* Paris: Organisation for Economic Cooperation
    and Development. Available from: www.oecd.org/about/
OECD (n.d. b) *About the OECD: History.* Paris: Organisation for Economic
    Cooperation and Development. Available from: www.oecd.org/about/
    history/
OECD (n.d. c) *About: What is PISA?* Paris: Organisation for Economic Cooperation
    and Development. Available from: www.oecd.org/pisa/aboutpisa/
OECD (1996a) *Thematic Review of Tertiary Education.* Paris: Organisation for
    Economic Cooperation and Development.
OECD (1996b) *Internationalization of Higher Education.* Paris: Organisation for
    Economic Cooperation and Development.
OECD (2004a) *Internationalisation and Trade in Higher Education.* Paris:
    Organisation for Economic Cooperation and Development.
OECD (2004b) *Quality Assurance and Recognition in Higher Education: The
    Cross-Border Challenge.* Paris: Organisation for Economic Cooperation and
    Development.
OECD (2005) *Guidelines in Quality Provision of Cross Border Higher Education.*
    Paris: Organisation for Economic Cooperation and Development.
OECD (2006a) *Four Future Scenarios for Higher Education.* Paris: Organisation
    for Economic Cooperation and Development.
OECD (2006b), *Education Policy Analysis 2006: Focus on Higher Education.*
    Paris: Organisation for Economic Cooperation and Development.
OECD (2008a) *Higher Education to 2030.* Paris: Organisation for Economic
    Cooperation and Development.
OECD (2008b) *Tertiary Education for the Knowledge Society,* Volume I. Paris:
    Organisation for Economic Cooperation and Development.
OECD (2009) *Higher Education to 2030,* Volume II. Paris: Organisation for
    Economic Cooperation and Development.
OECD (2012a) *AHELO Project Update – May 2012.* Paris: Organisation for
    Economic Cooperation and Development. Available from: www.oecd.org/
    dataoecd/8/26/48088270.pdf
OECD (2012b) *Approaches to Internationalisation and Their Implications for
    Strategic Management and Institutional Practice.* Paris: Organisation for
    Economic Cooperation and Development.
OECD (2015) *Education Policy Outlook: United Kingdom.* Paris: Organisation for
    Economic Cooperation and Development.
OECD (2016) *Building Skills for All: A Review of England, OECD Skills Studies.*
    Paris: Organisation for Economic Cooperation and Development.

OECD (2017a) *Skills Outlook 2017: Skills and Global Value Chains, Country Note* – United Kingdom. Paris: Organisation for Economic Cooperation and Development.

OECD (2017b) *Benchmarking Higher Education System Performance: Conceptual Framework and Data, Enhancing Higher Education System Performance*. Paris: Organisation for Economic Cooperation and Development.

OECD (2018a) *Secretary-General's Report to Ministers 2018*. Paris: Organisation for Economic Cooperation and Development.

OECD (2018b) *Preparing Our Youth for an Inclusive and Sustainable World: The OECD PISA Global Competence Framework*. Paris: Organisation for Economic Cooperation and Development.

OECD (2018c) *Enhancing Higher Education System Performance*. Paris: Organisation for Economic Cooperation and Development.

OECD (2018d) *Education Policy Outlook 2018: Putting Student Learning at the Centre*. Paris: Organisation for Economic Cooperation and Development.

Olds, K (2010, 1 August) The OECD's AHELO: a PISA for higher education? *Inside Higher Education*. Available from: www.insidehighered.com/blogs/globalhighered/oecds-ahelo-pisa-higher-education

Papadopoulos, G (1994) *Education 1960–1990*. Paris: Organisation for Economic Cooperation and Development.

Rinne, R, J Kallo, and S Hokka (2004) Too eager to comply? OECD education policies and the Finnish response. *European Educational Research Journal*, 3(2), 454–484.

Rizvi, F and B Lingard (2010) *Globalizing Education Policy*. London: Routledge.

Schuller, T and S Vincent-Lancrin (2009) OECD work on the internationalization of higher education: an insider perspective. In: RM Bassett and A Maldonado-Maldonado, eds. *International Organizations and Higher Education Policy: Thinking Globally, Acting Locally?* New York: Routledge.

Shahjahan, RA and LE Torres (2013) A "Global Eye" for teaching and learning in higher education: a critical policy analysis of the OECD's AHELO study. *Policy Futures in Education*, 11(5), 606–620.

UK Higher Education International Unit (2013) *UK Strategy for Outward Mobility*. London: Universities UK. Available from: www.universitiesuk.ac.uk/policy-and-analysis/reports/Documents/2014/UK-strategy-for-outward-mobility.pdf

UUKi (2017) *UK Strategy for Outward Student Mobility* 2017–2020. London: Universities UK International.

van der Wende, MC (2011) Global institutions: the organisation for economic co-operation and development. In: R King, S Marginson, and R Naidoo, eds. *Handbook on Globalization and Higher Education*. Cheltenham: Edward Elgar.

CHAPTER 6

Contesting student identities

Making sense of students' positioning in higher education policy

Adam Wright and Rille Raaper

Introduction

This chapter aims to trace and illustrate the interplay between different images of the student, constructed within, and in response to, policy discourses in higher education (HE) in England. We approach HE policy as something that gets interpreted and enacted within localities, making it open to contestation and change by those within the HE sector. This also means that policy effects on practices and individuals are always contextual, confirming the need to explore the ways in which students are positioned in contemporary policy discourses.

Recent policy reforms in English HE have leveraged an increasing number of market-oriented logics to university practices, such as choice, competition, performance, and satisfaction, that shape the opportunities and experiences of staff and students. As a consequence, a portrait has been produced of students as consumers. However, students manoeuvre within these complex policy settings and may shape, or impact on, policy agendas. In this chapter, students' political agency, by which we mean their ability to challenge and alter policy discourses and sound their own demands, is explored at the macro-level in terms of their engagement with government, the education sector, and the public, and at the micro-level in regard to their encounters with policy within their own institutions. As policy can influence and challenge identities and practices, we argue that interactions with education policy are rarely neutral. Most policy engagement becomes a political process, one which offers opportunities for contestation and change.

By discussing both the policy representation of students and students' response to HE policy, this chapter aims to provide a synthesis of student representation in a contemporary English HE setting. It supports professionals in navigating through a complex policy discourse and challenging unhelpful images of students while attempting to build stronger and more sustainable models of student engagement in which students and staff are effectively included and empowered.

Students in higher education policy discourse

The meanings of educational policies are not found in some pure form by analysing texts and speeches, but by interrogating the relationship between text/speech and wider social and historical contexts (Olssen, Codd, and O'Neill 2004). When addressing the question of students in HE policy, we must begin by understanding how the current positioning of the student relates to an evolving policy discourse in HE that fits (albeit not always neatly) within much wider political projects.

For policies to work, the discourse used to articulate them must be *performative*, in that it must lead people to act or to change the way they act to achieve some form of desired effect. To help achieve this, policy discourses construct identities for key stakeholders and position them as subjects of the discourse; in other words, as participants in a set of ideas and practices that make up the policy. It may seem unsurprising, then, that the student is identified as a key subject position in HE policy. Students are currently portrayed in policy discourse as actors who drive up educational standards by making informed choices, delivering feedback on their experience, and, when necessary, complaining when their experience fails to match up to expectations. But students have not always held such a key position in HE policy. Students have often been merely the beneficiaries of policy aims, such as an increase in university places, or packages of finance and support. What we have seen is a shift in the positioning of the student from a largely passive subject of policy to an extremely active subject.

Under the New Labour government (1997–2010), students became active in two senses. First, they were seen as contributors to the cost of HE, in order to fund a sustainable and more equitable system. This was characterised by a "partnership between students, government, business and universities" (DfES 2003). However, a second role for the student began to emerge within the policy discourse of New Labour: that of a student's choice between courses. While there remained a strong collaborative element, characterised by reference to the system as self-improving and often not (solely) to blame for its failings, the benefits of collaboration were not deemed sufficient to drive up standards on their own. Instead, students were given the role of driving up standards by choosing "good-quality courses" over others. In 2005, this market-oriented role for students was formalised in the creation of the National Student Survey (NSS) which allowed current students to deliver feedback on the quality of their course to help inform the choices of prospective students and, in turn, encourage institutions to improve their offer in order to compete.

Students, therefore, took on a dual identity under New Labour: as partners in creating and sustaining a fair system of HE, and as individual market actors, using their consumer power to drive institutions, through market competition, to improve their provision. This dual identity represented a larger split in New Labour's education policy between building a just and cohesive society, including through widening access to education and a commitment to lifelong learning, and delivering the skills needed for prosperity, in a knowledge-based, global economy. It was the latter, consumer positioning of the student that became the driving force behind the Conservative–Liberal Democrat coalition government's White Paper *Students at the heart of the system* (BIS 2011). The title itself suggests a central role for the student, and this role was identified as "well-informed students driving teaching excellence". This was to be achieved by positioning the student within an HE marketplace.

The student-as-consumer identity has been most fervently articulated through the policy discourse of the Conservative governments since 2015. The policy programme set out in the Green Paper *Fulfilling our potential* (BIS 2015) and the White Paper *Success as a knowledge economy* (BIS 2016) put an emphasis on market choice and competition in which the informed student-consumer played an active and central role. In *Success as a knowledge economy*, "student(s)" were mentioned 329 times as actors in HE, compared with only 58 mentions of "business(es) or employer(s)" and 16 mentions of academic staff. Students are imagined as the key actor, the catalyst for change, achieved through the delivery of greater market choice and competition. In a speech accompanying the 2015 Green Paper, Minister for Universities and Science Jo Johnson claimed that "competition … empowers students" (Johnson 2015). What is also interesting about this articulation is the way that the widening participation agenda is subsumed within the student-consumer identity. Students are no longer seen as partners in delivering a fairer system; institutions are subservient to the needs of the student-consumer, and through greater transparency and information about the backgrounds of applicants, choice and competition will drive social mobility (Callender and Dougherty 2018).

In parallel to the emergence of the student-as-consumer identity, a positioning of the student as a partner in HE has developed within the HE sector, without a clear articulation within government policy discourse. Policy as enacted through sector bodies like the Quality Assurance Agency for Higher Education (QAA) and the Higher Education Academy (HEA, since dissolved to become Advance HE) has tended to encourage the positioning of the student as an active partner in the development of teaching and learning, quality assurance, and institutional governance (see QAA 2018; Healey, Flint, and Harrington 2014). In Wales and Scotland, the student-as-partner mentality is perhaps even more embedded: the Wales Initiative for Student Engagement (WISE) was established in 2009 to share best practice on student engagement, and in 2013 it became Wise Wales and updated its mission "to achieve meaningful partnership between educators, students' unions and students across

Wales"; Scotland established a publicly funded agency, Student Participation in Quality Scotland (Sparqs) in 2003 to involve students in decisions about quality and governance of the learning experience, and in 2015 its name was changed to Student *Partnerships* in Quality Scotland. The development of the student-as-partner identity in England has appeared partly as a sector response to marketisation, led by the high-level engagement of the National Union of Students (NUS) with other sector bodies, particularly since the launch of the NUS *Manifesto for Partnership* in 2012.

However, this partnership identity, which fosters collaboration and co-production, has been threatened by the reforms of the Higher Education and Research Act 2017, and the antagonistic and often contradictory response of the student movement to them. Widespread opposition to the Teaching Excellence and Student Outcomes Framework (TEF) and the subsequent boycott of the 2017 National Student Survey, for instance, may well have made a student-engaged approach to regulation and quality assurance more difficult and, ultimately, less desirable.

Students within institutional policy enactment

English universities, like many other Western HE institutions, have been shaped by new forms of institutional governance approaches borrowed from the private sector. Informed by New Public Management (NPM), the reforms have aimed to reshape the relationships between private and public sectors, making the latter resemble the business world (Newman 2000). There has been a shift from collective forms of academic governance, and relative autonomy over research and teaching practices, to corporate-style leadership where academics are expected to meet centrally imposed performance targets. The shift towards marketisation of HE has created a situation where NPM is seen as essential for ensuring institutional competitiveness in various international and national league tables. League table positions are important for attracting research funding and demonstrating quality but, perhaps most importantly, for being able to attract new students. Students-as-consumers are expected to "shop" for a university and a degree programme based on various factors such as price, services provided, and reputation, revealed through numerous rank orders. In many of these league tables, student experience has become one of the metrics that enables differentiation of universities and their reputation. Sabri (2011, 657) argues that the phrase "the student experience" has "acquired the aura of a sacred utterance" where experience can be measured, quantified, and constantly improved. This focus on league tables and the associated market position has become an aim in itself, resulting in what Ball (2012, 34) describes as "governing by numbers". It also reflects the assumptions of "McKinseyism", where ever-increasing targets, permanent control over staff, and the culture of mistrust are seen as essential for increasing efficiency and productivity (Lorenz 2012).

NSS has become a particularly influential tool in measuring student experience and making it visible. Many league tables, and TEF, introduced in 2016, use NSS as one of the core metrics to evidence high-quality teaching. This, however, has received criticism from both universities and students who argue that quality teaching does not merely equal student satisfaction and vice versa. We also know that NSS can be manipulated, for example, by universities using incentives to encourage students to complete the survey, and students boycotting NSS to make a political point. NSS has become strongly associated with evidencing consumer satisfaction, feeding into a wider debate around the legal positioning of students-as-consumers.

The Consumer Rights Act 2015 provided the occasion for the clarification of universities' responsibilities to students under consumer law. In its guidance to universities, the Competition and Markets Authority (CMA) grounded the university and student consumer relationship in three core areas: information provision, terms and conditions, and complaints handling (CMA 2015). This conceptualisation of student experience as consumer satisfaction reflects an assumption that if students act as consumers, they will pressure universities to develop the highest-quality courses and academic practices (Naidoo and Williams 2015). It is also seen by government as a way to make universities comply with the student interest, a point that featured prominently in its White Paper *Success as a knowledge economy.* In the light of the CMA guidance, universities had to adjust their practices (see CMA 2017). Many institutions now employ or consult with legal compliance officers to ensure they act within the law. In addition, universities have started to add information on consumer rights on their websites and to produce new forms of communication with students. Many universities and their departments now hold dedicated "You said, we did" webpages to address and respond to student feedback. These initiatives aim to mediate potential tensions between the interests of universities and students, enabling the universities to demonstrate that the student voice is being taken seriously.

The cases above suggest that the relationship between HE institutions and students has been increasingly formalised and homogenised, often ignoring the uniqueness of educational processes, and the role of academics in facilitating learning and teaching. Universities have been made to comply with, and enforce, the idea of students-as-consumers. However, there is plenty of evidence to suggest that students do not necessarily perceive themselves as consumers, nor their education as a consumer transaction. A recent large-scale survey led by Universities UK suggests that consumerist policy discourses have had some, but limited, impact on the undergraduate student identity in the UK. According to the survey, 50 per cent of participants identified themselves as consumers of HE and, even then, this consumer relationship was seen as unique, relying on trust and collaboration rather than "shopping around" (UUK 2017).

Furthermore, academic research has identified that educational practices in HE (such as reliance on student active participation in seminar discussions) make it difficult for students to act as passive recipients of teaching; consumption goes hand in hand with production of education by students and staff in the classroom (Hoffman and Kretovics 2004). It could therefore be argued that the consumer identity is imposed on students, but little is known of its actual effect on student experiences. There is some evidence to suggest that students are incorporating consumerist views in terms of their expectations of value for money and employability but their relationship with academics and classroom practice goes beyond a simplistic consumer mentality (see Kandiko Howson and Mawer 2013). It is therefore more likely that the impact on student identity is subtle and context-dependent, rather than students straightforwardly adopting the consumer identity, as critics sometimes suggest.

While there is a mismatch between how students are positioned in national and institutional policies and in their own discourses, the widespread effects of consumerism on university education cannot be ignored. Marketisation encourages a one-sided relationship of institutional obligations towards students: to provide them with a "good" experience as opposed to intellectually challenging them and working together as partners. Student representative bodies are having to navigate this complexity in their efforts to represent the interests of students within their institution and in national policymaking.

The student as a subject of political contestation

In their guise as consumers, students have become one of the most important and active interest groups in the sector, and it is presumed that their rights to value for money and good experience need to be safeguarded. It is therefore unsurprising that within a consumerist setting in which students are active subjects, student politics has undergone a repositioning and students' unions, as central actors within this field, have become important stakeholders as representatives of student needs and interests in HE policy debates. Students' unions are often consulted on policy matters, including on the proposals leading to the Higher Education and Research Act 2017. But, simultaneously, the government is trying to mould students' unions into brokers for the market interests of students-as-consumers, limiting their wider collective political power. This has had clear implications on the behaviour of students' unions, which appear locked in the middle of the political conflict over student identity.

Given that the positioning of students has become highly complex in a consumerist sector, it would be naive to suggest that students have just become depoliticised, or that institutions or policymakers can point to a single, coherent "student voice" or "student experience". Instead, there seems to be increasing inconsistency between the ways in which politics and policies are spoken about and how students enact those views (Raaper 2018). Part of the complexity of student positioning is that students engage with policy at different levels: at the macro-level, engaging with government, the education sector, and the wider public; and at the micro-level, engaging in localised struggles within their own institution. At both levels, students can be engaged with both educational policies and wider political issues. With students' unions the boundaries between different levels and dimensions are not altogether clear. NUS often struggles to represent student politics at these different levels and scopes. Internal conflict emerges between those who wish to focus on the key issues for students on campus and those who seek to use the student movement as a vehicle for campaigning about national and international political issues.

We also know that consumer culture and the emphasis on individual rights have led to social fragmentation of group loyalties which, in turn, have resulted in an era of personalised politics focused on lifestyle choices and identity formation (see "Example one: safe space policies"). It could even be suggested that neither the existing macro-level representational model of student influence on HE policy, nor the traditional modes of political engagement within institutions, reflect the needs and interests of contemporary students and the formation of their political identity. Rather, the complex changes within the student population and their representative bodies deserve wider attention to be able to shift away from a normative understanding of what counts as political agency in an increasingly marketised HE sector.

Example one: safe space policies

Debates over safe spaces and trigger warnings provide an excellent example of contestation in HE where various drivers shape educational processes and agendas. For instance, the University of Cambridge has used trigger warnings to inform English Literature undergraduates about potentially disturbing content in Shakespeare plays *Titus Andronicus* and *The Comedy of Errors* (O'Connor 2017). The campaigns on "Rhodes must fall" and "Why is my curriculum White?" (see Abou El Magd 2016) have further exposed the tensions between universities' histories and the diversity and needs of the contemporary student population. Within student politics, these practices are seen as an important part of embracing diversity and challenging uneven power relations based on individual and group identities.

However, some criticise universities for packaging academic knowledge in certain protective ways with an aim to secure good student experience or public reputation. Others argue that students are undermining free expression and academic rigour because of oversensitivity, a claim which has led to their depiction as "snowflakes": an increasingly fragile generation of students who want to be safeguarded through their university education. Though grounded in very little actual evidence, the concept has been amplified through national media with growing number of articles with headlines such as "'Snowflake' generation of students' hostility to free speech revealed" (Turner 2018), and "Snowflake generation wants to exclude those who disagree" (Thomson and Sylvester 2017).

It is likely that marketisation discourses have been at play in both institutional and student articulations of this agenda in subtle ways. It might be that universities adopt safe-space policies and other procedures in order to eliminate any potential risk of pedagogical practices undermining the "consumer" experience or, alternatively, they may see this as a crucial part of a partnership model for engaging with an increasingly diverse student body. Furthermore, the positioning of students as consumers – in both policy and media – can result in students behaving in a more self-interested way, where individual gratifications and beliefs start outweighing democratic discussions over what counts as inclusive teaching and learning practices. It could therefore be argued that it is partly through marketisation discourses, not in opposition to them, that safe-space policies have gained ground.

As in any form of representative democracy, the relationship between the representatives and their constituents is elastic and often tenuous, although students' unions often claim to wholeheartedly represent the interests of students. Many students will not engage with a union and unions often find postgraduates, mature, part-time, and distance learners hard to engage (although many try very hard to do so). Representatives have their own priorities that may differ from the wider student body. Moreover, students' union officers are often expected to sit within governance structures of institutions, such as a university senate or council, without a mandate to negotiate on behalf of the student body – they are, on paper, there as individuals.

The student-consumer positioning has added further depth and difficulty to these conflicts. Identifying students as consumers is fortuitous for students' unions in a number of ways. The emphasis on the active role of the student has been seen as a new bargaining power, with unions taking up a "watchdog" role in ensuring student demands are met by institutions. When managed effectively, this has brought seemingly greater influence over the micro level, building stronger relationships with, and being treated as an insider by, their institution. In some cases, students' unions have followed the government logic of rearticulating the concept of student partnership under a consumerist framework and have ditched more significant (and difficult) models of co-production for more instrumentalist approaches that operationalise student feedback and complaints processes to improve outcomes. This has been seen most notably in response to TEF, as discussed in the next section.

Example two: TEF

TEF is a policy that highlights the contradiction between partner and consumer positionings. An outcomes-focused and metric-driven framework that is largely designed to provide better market information to students is framed by its opponents on the political left as part of an ongoing marketisation agenda. A more accurate description of TEF would be as a regulatory tool of the state to correct the market's failure to deliver adequate improvements to provision through competition. TEF, however, is not a simple policy to enact. For some, it is a welcome lever to pressure institutions to improve the student experience and internally, at some institutions, it has fostered even stronger models of partnership between students and management. It is also a source of antagonism between academic and professional staff, much like the Research Excellence Framework (REF) has become. It therefore sits as a site of political contestation at the institutional level and, within limits, institutions can rearticulate the demands of TEF to better fit their own agendas.

The 2017 boycott of NSS highlighted this contradiction within the student movement. NUS organised the boycott in response to the survey being used as a "core metric" for TEF, which had been intended to determine the level of tuition fee an institution could set. Many students' unions took part, particularly those in the Russell Group, leading to 12 institutions, including the Universities of Oxford and Cambridge, failing to meet the 50 per cent response-rate threshold required for results publication. However, several students' unions actively protested the boycott. They argued that NSS was an important bargaining tool for students and one of the best ways for students to lobby for change at their institution. They saw the boycott as a divisive tactic that would damage relations between students' unions and the institution.

These conflicts are also accompanied by disagreement over tactics. Direct action, both at the macro level (demonstrations, mass boycotts) and at the micro level (occupations, rent strikes, campus protests), is a favoured tactic of the political left of the student movement, although not exclusively. Other elements of the movement favour a more pragmatic approach and will use lobbying tactics, research-led campaigning, and formal and back-room negotiation to influence institutions, sector bodies, local, and national governments. Day and Dickinson (2018) argue that these tactical differences reflect longstanding divisions in the student movement which predate the current issues of marketisation and consumerism.

While students' unions have become important stakeholders at a national policy level, there is also evidence of changing dynamics between students' unions and their universities. Research has shown closer relationships between unions and senior management, and a tendency to employ an increasing number of professional non-elected officers to students' unions (Brooks, Byford, and Sela 2015). The strategic positioning of students' unions, both in terms of involvement in university governance and in provision of student services, allows institutions to demonstrate that the "student voice" is being taken seriously and student needs are accommodated (ibid.). It also allows a degree of shared accountability and deferred responsibility for aspects of the student experience, which may be adding pressure on unions to adopt a market-orientated strategy.

It is important for professional staff in HE to acknowledge this complex nature of student politics and that what goes on locally, on campus, is influenced by wider events and, importantly, by the policy discourses within HE. While it may seem at first glance to contradict much of the political rhetoric of student politics, students and their unions have not simply stood in firm opposition to marketisation. Their engagement with the student-as-consumer identity is not simply one of aversion, but instead has been assimilated and manipulated to achieve different aims and comes into conflict and contradiction with many other political identities. Never underestimate, however, the ability for individuals and groups to effectively apply cognitive dissonance and ignore such conflicts in day-to-day relationships. Student politics may well be complex, but it can function fairly effectively and consistently regardless.

How can higher education policy professionals respond?

This chapter has attempted to provide readers with an introduction to the issues and debates surrounding student identity in the context of HE policy and how these are enacted in institutions. Throughout the chapter we have attempted to draw out the development of an image of the student-as-consumer within policy that has led to changes in perception and behaviour both on the part of institutional actors and those involved in the student movement, including students' unions and, indeed, students themselves. At times, the student-as-consumer has challenged, even subsumed, the student-as-partner identity. We are left now to identify for the reader what we feel are the most important points to take away from this examination of student identity:

- First, it is crucial to acknowledge that identities are *contingent*: they are always contestable and open to change. We have shown how students can respond to their positioning within policy discourses in a variety of ways. They do not simply behave as consumers because they are told they are consumers. As a result, institutions must acknowledge this contingency of identity in their relationship with students and not make assumptions and generalisations about how students might identify or behave.

- Second, we must accept that students are becoming more and more *active* in HE policy. This active student identity is important for HE and cannot be ignored. There may be those who still advocate a return to more collegial forms of university governance where academic staff had greater autonomy and control over teaching and learning. This does not play well with either the consumer or partner images of students. Professional staff must find a way of harnessing the active identity of students in a way that brings mutual benefit without leading either students, academics, or administrators to feel disempowered.

- Third, and linked directly to the previous two points, our analysis has uncovered the role of political *agency*: the ability for individuals to act independently and transform the world around them. One must not forget that policies are not merely imposed upon us; in enacting policy we can reinterpret it to meet different needs and align with different principles and ideals. In this case, we must acknowledge not only our own agency but the agency of others, including students, to change education. Despite the complex nature of student politics, students and their unions are often adroit at navigating different levels and dimensions of policy to achieve positive results and build effective working relationships with institutions. Institutions should not be afraid to embrace this. The crucial thing is to find ways in which competing identities and interests can positively interact to find acceptable solutions and achieve tangible progress.

The practical application of this approach will depend on specific contexts, but we leave the reader with some potential places from where to start. The active identity of students can and should be harnessed in different ways, to ensure inclusion of a diversity of voices. It is critical for institutions to move away from the homogenised image of the student while also accepting that a complete individualisation and personalisation of practice is neither achievable nor desirable. This does not always require formalised processes. Instead, more open forums can be established to share ideas and ensure creative interactions between different stakeholders which develop trust and understanding. Feeding off the curiosity and dynamism of students, professional staff can find ways to be more creative and avoid cynical and conservative attitudes.

To further ensure professional staff develop an understanding of students as policy actors, training exercises can be developed which focus on putting staff in students' shoes. NUS has previously used role-playing exercises to train student representatives, allowing them to take on different roles of students and staff in a university. It encourages the representatives to think about the interests and concerns of those whom they are trying to influence, building understanding and empathy. Flipping this exercise for staff, allowing them to take on different student positionings, could be equally effective.

We believe that accounting for these points will help professional and academic staff in HE to build stronger and more productive relationships with students and challenge the narrow interpretations of student engagement within market-based policy discourses.

References

Abou El Magd, N (2016) Why is my curriculum White? – Decolonising the academy. London: National Union of Students. Available from: www.nusconnect .org.uk/articles/why-is-my-curriculum-white-decolonising-the-academy

Ball, SJ (2012) *Global Education Inc: New Policy Networks and the Neo-Liberal Imaginary*. London: Routledge.

BIS (2011) *Students at the Heart of the System*. London: Department for Business, Innovation and Skills.

BIS (2015) *Fulfilling Our Potential: Teaching Excellence, Social Mobility and Student Choice*. London: Department for Business, Innovation and Skills.

BIS (2016) *Success as a Knowledge Economy: Teaching Excellence, Social Mobility and Student Choice*. London: Department for Business, Innovation and Skills.

Brooks, R, K Byford, and K Sela (2015) The changing role of students' unions within contemporary higher education. *Journal of Education Policy*, 30(2), 165–181.

Callender, C and KJ Dougherty (2018) Student choice in higher education – reducing or reproducing social inequalities? *Social Sciences*, 7(10), 189.

CMA (2015) *Higher Education Providers: Consumer Law. 60-Second Summary*. London: Competition and Markets Authority. Available from: www.gov. uk/government/uploads/system/uploads/attachment_data/file/411392/HE_ providers_60ss.pdf

CMA (2017) *Higher Education: Consumer Protection Review*. London: Competition and Markets Authority. Available from: www.gov.uk/cma-cases/ consumer-protection-review-of-higher-education

Day, M and J Dickinson (2018) *David Versus Goliath: The Past, Present and Future of Students' Unions in the UK*. Oxford: Higher Education Policy Institute.

DfES (2003) *The Future of Higher Education*. London: Department for Education and Skills.

Healey, M, A Flint, and K Harrington (2014) *Engagement Through Partnership: Students as Partners in Learning and Teaching in Higher Education*. York: Higher Education Academy.

Hoffman, KD and MA Kretovics (2004) Students as partial employees: a metaphor for the student-institution interaction. *Innovative Higher Education*, 29(2), 103–120.

Johnson, J (2015, 9 September) *Higher Education: Fulfilling our Potential.* Available from: www.gov.uk/government/speeches/higher-education-fulfilling-our-potential

Kandiko Howson, CB and M Mawer (2013) *Student Expectations and Perceptions of Higher Education.* London: King's Learning Institute.

Lorenz, C (2012) 'If you're so smart, why are you under surveillance?' Universities, neoliberalism, and new public management. *Critical Inquiry* 38(3), 599–629.

Naidoo, R and J Williams (2015) The neoliberal regime in English higher education: charters, consumers and the erosion of the public good. *Critical Studies in Education*, 56(2), 208–223.

Newman, J (2000) Beyond the new public management? Modernizing public services. In: J Clarke, S Gewirtz, and E McLaughlin, eds. *New Managerialism, New Welfare?* London: Sage, pp. 45–61.

NUS (2012) *A Manifesto for Partnership.* London: National Union of Students.

O'Connor, R (2017) Cambridge University students given trigger warnings for Shakespeare plays. *The Independent.* Available from: www.independent.co.uk/arts-entertainment/books/news/cambridge-university-trigger-warnings-shakespeare-plays-titus-andronicus-mary-beard-academics-a8008456.html

Olssen, M, J Codd and A O'Neill (2004) *Education Policy: Globalization, Citizenship and Democracy.* London: Sage.

QAA (2018) Chapter B5: *Student Engagement, UK Quality Code for Higher Education.* Gloucester: Quality Assurance Agency for Higher Education.

Raaper, R (2018). Students' unions and consumerist policy discourses in English higher education. *Critical Studies in Education (online first)*, 1–17.

Sabri, D (2011) What's wrong with "the student experience"? *Discourse: Studies in the Cultural Politics of Education*, 32(5), 657–667.

Thomson, A, and R Sylvester (2017) Snowflake generation want to exclude those who disagree. *The Times.* Available from www.thetimes.co.uk/article/snowflake-generation-want-to-exclude-those-who-disagree-wt80gg9fw

Turner, C (2018) "Snowflake" generation of students' hostility to free speech revealed. *The Telegraph.* Available from: www.telegraph.co.uk/education/2018/06/28/snowflake-generation-students-hostility-free-speech-revealed/

UUK (2017) *Education, Consumer Rights and Maintaining Trust: What Students Want from Their University.* London: Universities UK. Available from: www.universitiesuk.ac.uk/policy-and-analysis/reports/Documents/2017/education-consumer-rights-maintaining-trust-web.pdf

PART 2

Regulation and the role of government

CHAPTER 7

Higher education policymaking from the government's perspective

Iain Mansfield

Introduction

This chapter will consider higher education (HE) policymaking from the government's perspective, including the formal and informal powers of ministers, the role of the civil service, and observations on the interaction of government with the HE sector. It will focus primarily on the departmental level, considering what can be achieved by a Minister of State, or Secretary of State, taking into account the relationship with other parts of government and the sector's regulators, and how the distinct nature of the HE sector both imposes constraints and provides opportunities for realising ministerial ambitions. Finally, it will consider the extent to which the maxim, "We always overestimate the change that will occur in the next two years and underestimate the change that will occur in the next ten" (Gates 1996) applies to how much a minister is able to achieve in HE policymaking.

The structure and nature of power

Compared to many other areas of the Department for Education's (DfE) remit, the government's ability to intervene directly in the HE sector is extremely constrained. Ministers and officials coming from schools policy are often astonished to discover that they have little power to tell universities which students to take, to influence the structure and content of academic programmes, or to control the standard for which classes of degrees are awarded. Ministers' powers to give direction to the Office for Students (OfS) are constrained by the requirement to have regard to institutional autonomy prescribed by the Higher Education and Research Act of 2017 (HERA), and OfS's actions are similarly constrained. Although the HERA gave OfS considerably more powers to intervene in the affairs of individual providers than its predecessors, by means of the imposition of "conditions of registration", these powers remain limited both by specific protections for matters such as admissions and standards, as well as a broader duty to have regard to institutional autonomy – and, of course, remain under the control of OfS, rather than under the control of ministers or departmental officials. The nature of these constraints in both law and custom will be explored further.

The factors that influence the ability to effect change are determined primarily by two considerations: the tier of power upon which that change operates, and the resources available, in particular the level of financial resource and whether or not time is devoted for primary legislation.

Tiers of power

- **Prime Minister and Chancellor level:** While many matters formally require assent from the Prime Minister's office at No. 10 Downing Street, through the process of Cabinet Clearance or due to central control over the government's legislative programme, matters at this tier will be of direct interest to the Prime Minister or Chancellor due to their impact on wider government polices, their impact on public finances, or the level of public controversy. A departmental minister's views on such matters will therefore become secondary to the outcome, though they may continue to have significant input and influence. As (fictional) MP Roger Quaife puts it in the classic Whitehall novel:

> Remember, these are going to be real decisions … there won't be many of them, they're only too real. People like you, sitting outside, can influence them a bit, but you can't make them. Your scientists can't make them. Civil servants can't make them. So far as that goes, as a Junior Minister, I can't make them.
>
> (Snow 1966)

    Issues that operate at this level include the student funding regime; student migration; or major changes to the overall settlement between government and providers, such as the transformation of polytechnics to universities in the Further and Higher Education Act of 1992. Hypothetically, potential future initiatives, such as an attempt to roll back institutional autonomy in a major area such as admissions, would also fall into this area.
- **Departmental:** At the level of the DfE rests the ability to shape the system as a whole, either through legislation (primary or secondary) or via means such as directions, guidance letters, or less formal influence over OfS. Through ministerial speeches and media activity, the department has the means to put items on the agenda, to galvanise action, and to shape the broader climate or policy. Without legislation, this can include determining the relative balance between pots of funding, prioritisation of issues such as mental health

or grade inflation or influence over regulatory tools such as the Research Excellence Framework (REF) or Teaching Excellence and Student Outcomes Framework (TEF); with legislation comes the ability to initiate greater changes, such as to alter fundamentally the system architecture, introduce new regulations such as those relating to fair access and widening participation, or to bring for-profit providers into the HE system. Direct intervention in the affairs of individual institutions is highly limited.

- **Regulator:** In the absence of primary legislation, arguably the most power rests at the tier of the regulator, particularly since the creation of OfS. At this tier rest the final decisions on how much grant is allocated to individual institutions, to operate instruments such as the TEF and broader quality assurance system, to make individual decisions about institutions, and to intervene directly through specific conditions of regulation, fines, the threat of deregistration, as well as softer interventions. Significant power also resides at the regulatory level to initiate programmes or research, such as that in "learning gain"; to convene task forces or review initiatives; to focus sector attention on certain issues; to shape the agenda of other bodies such as the Quality Assurance Agency for Higher Education (QAA); and to work with devolved nations on cross-UK matters. Even where an initiative is devised at the departmental level, due to the greater operational budget, expertise, and levels of staffing resource that reside in the regulator, it is usually left to the regulator to carry it out (in 2018, DfE had fewer than 200 staff working on HE, while OfS had around 400).
- **Sector agencies:** More than many sectors, HE is marked by a degree of co-regulation, with sector-owned agencies taking on roles that elsewhere would be played by government bodies. Though less influential than they were in their heyday of the early 2000s, bodies such as the QAA, Advance HE (an amalgam of the Higher Education Academy, Equality Challenge Unit and Leadership Foundation for Higher Education), and the Higher Education Statistics Agency (HESA) continue to play an important part in influencing the broader environment and narratives that shape the sector. None of these bodies is classed as being part of the public sector, though government can exert influence via funding, regulatory pressure, and, in the case of the QAA and HESA, through the powers in HERA to make formal designation of quality and data bodies.
- **Universities:** Due to the level of autonomy, individual vice-chancellors have significant control over their own institutions, though limited influence over the system as a whole. Individual universities are therefore free to pursue their own, highly varied, trajectories, and to respond to the common pressures imposed by regulation, demographic trends, and competitive pressures in widely disparate ways.

It should be emphasised that the tier of power does not depend on whether or not a matter requires legislation, though this may be correlated. HERA, for example, operated primarily at the departmental tier, and was initiated and driven by departmental ministers – though it was naturally, in certain areas, constrained by the views of No. 10.

Resources

The two principal resources that determine the options available to a minister are money and legislation. Money is easily explained: a looser funding environment allows the creation of funds and initiatives, the financial incentivising of desired behaviour, and the ability to cushion the blow to institutions that may lose out in any policy initiatives. It is significantly more popular, for example, to offer additional funding for provision of STEM (science, technology, engineering, and maths) courses than to remove funding from non-STEM courses, even if both might have a similar effect on the behaviour of institutions. Furthermore, a constrained funding environment is likely to necessitate difficult decisions, reducing the goodwill that may be required to pass other reforms. The financial position of the sector is also a factor: it is easier to make difficult decisions if it will "only" result in universities cutting back on certain activities; it becomes significantly more challenging if there is a real risk of courses or universities closing.

Legislation is a rare phenomenon. There have been only three major HE Acts since 1990 – the Further and Higher Education Act (1992), the Higher Education Act (2004), and the Higher Education and Research Act (2017) – and no minister can count on one: David Willetts, as a minister with a clear, government-backed reform agenda, lost his bill slot in 2012 after the undergraduate tuition fee increase to £9,000 caused such controversy that the Coalition Government became unwilling to contemplate further HE legislation. Legislation is not a blank cheque – the contents of a bill are limited by the parliamentary arithmetic, the government's appetite for controversy, and other matters – but it dramatically increases the options available to a minister.

"Ministry policy"

Initiatives of departmental ministers are mediated through the activities of civil servants. Without clear ministerial direction, civil servants will typically continue to pursue "ministry policy"; responding in an evolutionary manner to ongoing events, but without questioning the fundamental principles under which they are operating (for example, whether or not more people going to university is a good idea). Ministry policy comprises a combination between the principles espoused by the last minister who gave strong and clear direction upon the subject in question on the one hand, and received sector wisdom on the other, and typically consists of a large quantity of well-researched evidence and statistics, combined with a generous dose of unquestioned assumptions. It is important to recognise the existence of "ministry policy" in policymaking and public affairs: not only will it typically be briefed to new ministers as fact and determine policy advice in any area where the minister has not yet given clear direction, but it comprises a reservoir of inertia that must be overcome, either by a minister seeking to effect change, or by a public affairs officer seeking to influence policy.

Departmental and regulatory balance

One of the most significant elements in HE policy is the relationship between DfE and the regulator, formerly the Higher Education Funding Council for England (Hefce) and now OfS. While OfS is the newer organisation, with some differences in its statutory duties, it is likely that the relationship with the department will continue to be subject to similar pressures and ambiguities. While DfE may issue guidance to OfS, in nearly all circumstances OfS need only pay regard to this: it is not bound to follow it. While HERA contains provisions for the Secretary of State to direct OfS, this requires secondary legislation; similar provisions in the Further and Higher Education Act (1992) were never used. In reality, the relationship is typically characterised by high levels of negotiations, with both parties having a strong interest in maintaining alignment. Guidance letters are shared and negotiated between officials at the two organisations – though ministers have the final say – and strong lines of communication ensure that both organisations have a full understanding of the priorities and concerns of the decision-makers in each body. There is usually a tacit understanding that the minister's political statements may be moderated and made practical by the regulator, and equally that the regulator will not take actions that fly in the face of the minister's principal objectives. This relationship is a core feature of the arm's-length nature of HE regulation, and managing it well is an essential skill for ministers, civil servants, and OfS staff who wish to achieve their strategic objectives.

In practice, the exact level at which decisions sit will be impacted by a number of factors, including ministerial trust (the more confident a minister feels in the regulator's leadership, the more they are likely to delegate), ministerial priorities (ministers will want more control over the policies most important to them), and, last but perhaps most important, the personalities, capabilities, and attitudes of the individuals involved in both organisations. Together, these mean that – except at the extremes – there is no hard and fast rule as to where decisions will be made, and the principal locus on a matter such as access and participation may drift back and forth between the department and the regulator over time. For those outside government seeking to influence policymaking, this ambiguity means there is simply no substitute for engagement, as the most appropriate locus to influence will vary on a case-by-case basis. The one occasion on which the pendulum swings decisively towards ministers is when legislation is being passed, for such matters lie entirely within the government's, or parliament's, control – though the regulator may, and likely will, be consulted. Once the landscape has been reshaped and the legislative changes made, it will, however, typically fall to the regulator to implement the legislation, causing the pendulum to swing back once more.

Interfaces and dependencies

Like all policy areas, HE policy relates to many other areas across government. This chapter will not consider these in depth; however, the principal areas are typically:

- **Science and research:** Both HE and research are core to most universities, though the relative importance of each varies.
- **Regional and industrial policy:** Universities make a high contribution to the UK's economic activity, as employers, as innovators, and as generators of knowledge. Many play a pivotal role in the economy of their city or region.
- **Further education (FE):** Many FE colleges offer HE programmes and many universities offer courses at qualification Levels 4 and 5 (equivalent to the first two years of an undergraduate degree) or adult learning or foundation programmes which are below degree level. Different funding and legislative regimes can mean that very similar courses are funded and regulated in entirely different ways.
- **Adult skills policy:** The retraining and upskilling of adults are often seen as essential to maintaining the UK's future productivity. Universities are likely to have an important role in doing this.

Over the last 20 years both departmental and ministerial portfolios have varied in such a way as to move each of these policy areas administratively closer to or further from the HE brief.

Finally, it is important to remember that HE policy is a devolved matter, as are most of the matters above, with the exception of research. The differences between the systems have been steadily increasing since the beginning of the twenty-first century, but the desire to maintain a degree of harmony across the system, not least in terms of protecting its international reputation, imposes a countervailing policy pressure. The extent to which a minister or OfS is willing to diverge, if necessary, from the other nations of the UK on a particular policy is a matter worth considering explicitly at the beginning of the policy process.

Constraints

In addition to the constraints that impact upon any area of public policy-making, HE is subject to a specific set of additional constraints. Some of the most important of these are now detailed.

Institutional autonomy

As has been discussed, institutional autonomy is protected by law, both by specific protections for matters such as admissions and standards, as well as a broader duty for OfS to have regard to institutional autonomy. In addition to the legislative protections, the fact that, structurally, ministers can primarily impact upon the sector only through arm's-length bodies, combined with the history of co-regulation and the cultural expectation of autonomy, all serve to limit the extent to which ministers can directly impact the sector, particularly if they wish to do so without adverse comment in the press. Not even securing a bill allows a minister to circumvent the tradition of institutional autonomy. During the passage of HERA the perceived reduction in autonomy came under strong attack in the House of Lords, as well as repeated criticism in papers as diverse as the *Financial Times*, *Telegraph*, and *Guardian*, among others, despite the encroachments upon autonomy being relatively modest and leaving the core protections unchanged. Ultimately, the Government was forced to offer additional legislative safeguards on institutional autonomy, as well as revising the wording in other areas of concern, such as on standards. Similarly, in the Higher Education Act (2004) which introduced the Office for Fair Access (Offa), the legislation was carefully crafted to largely respect institutions' traditional autonomy in determining admissions, in particularly imposing a duty on the Director for Fair Access to protect the freedom of institutions to determine the criteria for the admission of students and apply those criteria. These protections were carried over in the HERA when the role of Offa was incorporated into OfS.

Timescales

The academic year and the length of the student application cycle mean that any major change takes time to introduce. Considering school-leavers, a major change that is announced in, for example, 2025 would be advertised to applicants applying that year, who would not start until 2026 and not gradu-ate until 2029. When one considers that many policies typically take at least a year to develop through consultation – and may take significantly longer if legislation is required – the time between first conception of a policy and an actual impact upon students may easily be three or more years, and upon graduates by six or seven years, even if all goes well. Pilots and trials simi-larly are constrained by the necessity of accommodating the academic year. In contrast, the typical tenure of a Universities Minister in recent times has been less than two years (between the 2010 General Election and the end of 2018 there were five: David Willetts, Greg Clark, Jo Johnson, Sam Gyimah, and Chris Skidmore). Unless a minister can be confident that their successor will take forward their reforms, this places significant constraints upon what can be achieved.

Influence

The HE sector possesses a unique confluence of factors that combine to make it highly influential beyond its apparent strength:

- A high economic importance, in terms of GDP, employment, and bal-ance of trade. The representative body Universities UK estimates that universities generate more than £73 billion a year in output for the British economy, contribute nearly 3 per cent of UK GDP, and generate more than 750,000 jobs.
- Mass involvement by the population: many people have either been to uni-versity or have children who wish to go,
- Connected, highly influential individuals – both distinguished academics and university chancellors.

All of these must be taken into account by a minister seeking to effect change. There are not many sectors which can bring out mass marches in the street (via the students' union movement), command over 50 members in the House of Lords, gain column inches in the major newspapers, and, perhaps most sig-nificantly of all, have direct access to senior figures at No. 10 or the Treasury.

Left-leaning

A particular challenge for Conservative or centrist Labour governments is the left-leaning nature of academia, both amongst academics and students (Morgan 2017; HEPI 2017). This manifests itself in a broad range of areas, from attitudes to private sector involvement, marketisation, and consumerisation to cultural attitudes to issues such as class, race, and gender. Such attitudes affect not only the degree of grassroots sectoral opposition to centre-right policies but also the broader nature of how debates are framed. For example, debates on access and attainment are often framed in traditionally left-wing language and tend to focus heavily on equality of outcome (even if ostensibly worded in terms of equality of opportunity). Similarly, a scepticism about rankings and hierarchies, an unwillingness to perceive any courses as poor quality, and the way in which even those who advocate for better conditions for students are typically unwilling to use the language of consumer rights or the market, are all ways in which the policy framing within the HE sector is shaped from a left-of-centre perspective. For one seeking to influence higher education policy, whether or not such views are "correct" is irrelevant; what is relevant; however, is to recognise that left-wing policies are more likely to find fertile ground for acceptance than right-wing ones.

Non-independence of research

In most areas of public policy, those carrying out research are from outside the groups who will be affected. While their views may vary greatly, they bring an outside perspective that serves to challenge internal narratives and opinions that are rarely questioned within the sector under scrutiny. In HE, the majority of researchers on the subject will, as academics, be part of the system they are studying. This is an inevitable consequence of the fact that most research is done in universities; however, it has the unfortunate consequence of making it more difficult to obtain perspectives that are not heavily influenced by the prevailing attitudes and "common wisdom" of the sector they are trying to study. Indeed, it is noticeable that many of the most impactful and influential pieces of research in recent years have been conducted by those who are not formally educational researchers – for example by David Palfreyman on the future of the university, by Gervas Huxley on contact hours, or by Phil Newton and Michael Draper on essay mills (at the time of writing, Palfreyman is the bursar of an Oxford College; Huxley is in an economics faculty; Newton in a faculty of medicine; Draper in a faculty of law) – or by think-tanks such as the Higher Education Policy Institute – with its highly influential student experience survey – rather than by the much larger body of scholars formally tasked with researching HE policy.

The consequences are three-fold. First, and counter-intuitively from the viewpoint of a policy official, consensus, group-think, and unexamined premises are significantly more common within the HE policymaking spaces than in most other policy areas. Second, unlike in other areas, it is more difficult for government to get high-quality, impartial sources of research and evidence from outside the very group that their policies are trying to impact. Finally, from the sector's perspective, it can be more difficult to sway critics with research, as they will understandably be sceptical of it. This often-over-looked fact is a major challenge for government: although any sector is subject to vested interests and unconscious bias, only in HE are those same people writing the research.

Effecting change

Given these constraints, how can a minister effect change? In the short term, a minister's position offers an excellent position from which to raise awareness of issues and place them on the agenda: from Gordon Brown raising concerns about Laura Spence and access to Oxbridge, to Jo Johnson campaigning against grade inflation, a minister raising an issue will help ensure it gets national airtime and attention. Similarly, where a minister wishes to address a specific matter that does not contradict the prevailing pressures of the sector, they may have some success: campaigns on mental health, narrowing the attainment gap for black students, and the experiences of students with disabilities are all areas where a focus by ministers has had little difficulty in raising the matter up the sector's agenda. Such actions, however, rarely impact upon the longer-term structure and dynamics of the system.

For a minister to be effective at driving forward long-term change, more is needed. Though individual institutions are autonomous, the HE system as a whole is highly responsive to incentives, both those imposed by government (for example funding or regulation) and those imposed by the external world. These deep structural factors tend to predominate over short-term initiatives, whether those be ministerial announcements or vice-chancellors' whims. Rather like an ideal gas, the system can therefore – in principle – be modelled and shaped at a systemic level, even if the behaviour of individual universities cannot be controlled. It transpires, therefore, that for long-term change to be effective, it must be delivered at the systemic level.

How, then, can this systemic change be achieved? First, it is important to recognise unintended consequences. Government notoriously failed to predict that almost all universities would charge £9,000 when the fee cap was raised to this level; similarly, the explosive growth of unconditional offers (Baker 2018) – a rational response to the removal of student number caps combined with a demographic dip – also failed to be predicted. Both of these also demonstrate how, despite widespread criticism, systemic pressures will dominate over other encouragements and stimulations to change. On the other hand, there have been successful efforts by government to introduce systemic change. The Research Selectivity Exercise, now the REF, has, since its introduction in the 1980s, successfully driven both a concentration in UK research and the intended increase in international excellence; similarly, the access and widening participation initiatives introduced in 2004 have ensured that access is now a core part of every university's activities and firmly embedded in the sector's culture. Two more recent initiatives, the increase in private providers begun by David Willetts and the introduction of the TEF by Jo Johnson, are similarly deliberate attempts to shape the system on a systemic level, though it is still too soon to tell whether or not they will be successful.

Effecting systemic change does not necessarily require primary legislation. Legislation, in fact, is no guarantee of success – though of course it may help, can expand the options available, and will increase a minister's influence over the regulator. Successfully achieving this degree of change will typically require consideration of the following factors:

- **Focus:** There are only so many areas in which major change can be driven forward at once. Choose areas, focus upon them, and drive them to successful completion, or change will devolve into transitory interventions and initiatives.
- **Know what's important:** All elements of the reform will likely be opposed by someone. Understanding which elements are key to success will allow a minister to make concessions without compromising their key objectives. For those outside government, understanding which areas the government sees as core is important to ensure effective influencing.
- **Make use of unexpected events:** As in any policy area, unexpected things happen, whether that is No. 10 taking an interest in a particular area, a media firestorm, a university or department in crisis, or a major review. The ability of a minister to make use of such events to implement their own, pre-existing, policy agenda, rather than being buffeted by the winds of others, can be critical to success.
- **Use the sector's diversity:** Other than on a very small number of topics (for example, the position in favour of a benign migration regime for international students) the sector will have a diverse range of views. This manifests itself not just in the diversity of mission groups, but in the variation of views within each group. The sector's highly fissiparous nature can be used effectively to gain support for and neutralise opposition to government policy. A good senior civil servant or experienced Universities Minister should have a clear understanding of the views of at least 50 or more influencers (for example individual vice-chancellors) within the sector.
- **Don't procrastinate:** As has been discussed earlier, the tenure of a Universities Minister is likely to be limited. Arguing for delay, and then hoping the minister in question will have been moved before a decision has to made, is one of the most effective tactics the sector can deploy to block policy it dislikes, effective in part because it can often be made to sound so reasonable.

- **Overcome inertia:** "Ministry policy", or inertia, can delay or subvert any change. Clear and repeated communication of objectives and priorities is the most important way in which a minister can overcome this, as is finding and empowering champions (in either the department or the regulator) who are able and willing to drive forward the change desired.
- **Shore up support:** It is difficult for a minister simultaneously to take on students, academics, and university leaders. Ideally, policies will be designed to win the support – or at least avoid the outright opposition – of at least one of these groups. Similarly, controversial policies need to have their vocal supporters outside the sector, for example with the wider public or the business community, if a minister wishes to retain support for their policies within government.
- **Lock in constituents:** To preserve systemic change, an effective policy will create a group of constituents who benefit from it and will argue for its preservation once the minister in question has gone. Whether vice-chancellors benefitting from £9,000 fees, Gold-rated TEF providers, or independent providers who now have a clear stake in the system, such constituents do not guarantee a policy will last, but they certainly help.

Conclusion

HE policymaking is subject to a wide range of specific circumstances and pressures, in particular those related to the arm's-length nature of regulation and institutional autonomy. At any time, the dynamic of power between central departments, DfE, and the current regulator will vary, increasing the challenge of shaping and influencing short-term policymaking. In the longer term, however, the system is highly responsive to incentives, which dominate in their effect over short-term initiatives. While these can be difficult to influence and to shape, successful endeavours will be highly effective at driving long-term, systemic change. In HE policymaking, therefore, it is particularly true that "We always overestimate the change that will occur in the next two years and underestimate the change that will occur in the next ten" (Gates 1996).

References

Baker, S (2018, 29 November) Two-thirds of applicants with unconditional offers missed grades. *Times Higher Education*. Available from: www.timeshighereducation.com/news/two-thirds-applicants-unconditional-offers-missed-grades

Gates, B (1996) *The Road Ahead*. London: Penguin.

HEPI (2017, 4 May) *Students Support Labour but Don't Trust Them on Fees, According to HEPI/YouthSight Poll.* Oxford: Higher Education Policy Institute. Available from: www.hepi.ac.uk/2017/05/04/4081/

Morgan, J (2017, 1 June) General election 2017: 54% backing for Labour in THE poll. *Times Higher Education.* Available from: www.timeshighereducation. com/news/general-election-2017-54-per-cent-backing-for-labour-in-poll

Snow, CP (1966) *Corridors of Power.* Harmondsworth: Penguin Books.

CHAPTER 8

Lessons from the legislative process

How representative groups shape government policy and legislation

William Hammonds and Chris Hale

Introduction

The focus of this chapter is on Universities UK's (UUK) role as an interest group seeking to influence policy change and legislation in higher education (HE). It does this by looking at how UUK sought to influence the creation of a new regulatory regime for HE in England.[1] The chapter examines UUK's engagement with the policy cycle, from early debates on the need for reform, the Green and White Papers, through to the passing of the Higher Education and Research Act 2017 and into implementation. The chapter is structured around four sections that cover key elements of the policy change process (see Figure 8.1). The first section examines the need for legislation, including the regulatory gaps following the 2012 HE funding reforms. The second explores how UUK's role as a membership organisation made up of shared and diverse interests shaped its priorities and positions. The third examines UUK's influencing strategies and tactics, and the fourth examines where UUK influenced the outcomes of the Act. The chapter concludes with final reflections on influencing policy and legislation.

The chapter is primarily concerned with UUK's role as an interest group that seeks to influence policy. It is less concerned with the merits or otherwise of the changes themselves beyond UUK's priorities in the process. The chapter illustrates how UUK's role, as an interest group, is best understood as a process of negotiation that required a careful navigation of trade-offs and political capital. Ultimately UUK sought to advance its members' priorities by understanding the Government's agenda and its political constraints and by working to advance areas of common interest. The authors are writing in a personal capacity and this article represents their personal understanding of the process and the strategy that was employed by UUK. It is not a formal evaluation of UUK's success or otherwise and, while it includes some reflections, it is left up to the reader to draw their own conclusions.

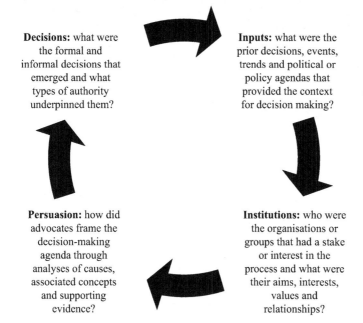

Figure 8.1 Theoretical model of the decision-making process (Hammonds 2018).

Engaging with and shaping an emerging reform agenda

UUK's engagement with this period of HE regulatory reform and legislation can be traced from the 2012 changes in the new funding regime for universities in England. The new fees-based system represented a fundamental departure from the arrangements that had been in place since the early 1990s. HE institutions in England had been primarily regulated through accountability for receipt of funding from the then Higher Education Funding Council for England (Hefce). This was underpinned by the Further and Higher Education Act 1992 and given expression through mechanisms such as the Memorandum of Assurance and Accountability which established the conditions of accountability for universities in receipt of public funding (Hefce 2017). Hefce's role under the 1992 Act was to secure accountability for use of public funds, including that funded provision met certain quality thresholds, and to support broad policy objectives through use of funding. However, Hefce's regulatory levers and accountability mechanisms were significantly weakened by the shift from public funding to the new fee- and income-contingent loan system. Regulated public grant income decreased for many providers and the existent legislative underpinnings did not allow Hefce to directly apply conditions to the increasingly significant income received by institutions through the student support system.

The new fees regime and government policy increasingly emphasised direct accountability between student and providers, rather than directly to government via Hefce. This recognised a shift in "who pays", while also promoting student choice to drive competition with the aim of enhancing quality and value for money across the system, largely defined around student satisfaction and employment outcomes. In addition, a growth in new entrants to the system was outside Hefce's direct jurisdiction, which resulted in an increasingly fragmented and uneven regulatory system. Alternative providers not in receipt of public funding could apply to the Department for Business, Innovation and Skills (BIS) to have specific courses designated for student support. From 2012, eligible students enrolled on courses designated for student support were able to access fee loans up to £6,000 per year alongside the standard maintenance loan package, an increase from the previous limit of £3,000; this led to a notable increase in the number of students enrolled on designated courses which subsequently led to enquiries by the National Audit Office that found significant concerns about the integrity and quality of some providers offering designated courses.

The political appetite to introduce new legislation at the time was limited. This was largely due to the political fallout within the Coalition Government from the 2012 increase in tuition fees. Despite setting out several challenges in a 2011 White Paper, instead of enacting a new regulatory regime the government implemented several workarounds to manage the risks in the system (BIS 2011). These included establishing the Regularity Partnership Group (RPG) between 2012 and 2015 and a voluntary agreement (AID: Agreement on Institutional Designation) between the sector, government, and regulator to extend Hefce's accountability powers to access to student support package (Hefce 2015a; 2015b). UUK actively worked with the RPG and led the development of the AID based on a collective responsibility and mutual interest in ensuring the system could still function. Through this work within UUK there was a growing recognition of a practical need for updating of legislation and coming to a longer-term and sustainable solution. The RPG and AID were sustained by the willingness on all sides, including sector and government agencies, to work to manage the resultant gaps. However, it was unsustainable in the long run, particularly as it could not meaningfully accommodate new alternative providers who had not previously been Hefce funded but who enjoyed enhanced access to the student support system after 2012.

This situation led to the first strategic trade-off for UUK. On the one hand, there was the need for new legislation to address the gaps in the regulatory system and the risks that this posed to students and the integrity of the sector as a whole. However, this was tempered across the UUK membership by the risks of opening up a legislative process that could lead to government overreaching its role to undermine institutional autonomy and pursue undesirable policy outcomes. It was in this context that UUK established a small working group, led by Professor Simon Gaskell, then President and Principal of Queen Mary University of London, to examine these issues. This group was tasked with exploring options for a new regulatory system and developing a way forward where there wasn't an obvious consensus. The working group format was an opportunity to examine the issues in depth, including evidence from external individuals and groups, while also enabling a vice-chancellor to lead the issue on behalf of UUK. The group reported in early 2015 and called for the establishment of a new lead regulator – to be called the Council for Higher Education England – with a single "gateway" register of all providers that would be more focused on student protection and accountability, including provisions for supporting institutional or course closures (UUK 2015).

When proposals for legislation were finally set out in a Green Paper, following the 2015 General Election victory for the Conservative Party, it set out plans for the Office for Students (OfS) and a new register. The ideas of a lead regulator and register, with legislative underpinnings, were consistent with Gaskell. However, where Gaskell's proposals envisaged a body with responsibility for the system, OfS was proposed with a narrow focus on the interest of students and an emphasis on competition. However, themes such as protection of students, academic autonomy, collaboration, and sector ownership of quality and standards can be traced from these discussions. Through the Gaskell report UUK was able to position itself strategically as a significant voice on regulatory reform with constructive proposals that addressed the core challenges, but this was only the start of a process with significant challenges ahead for influencing an evolving policy agenda and maintaining a coherent sector voice.

Priorities for UUK as a membership organisation

The Gaskell report played an important role in aligning UUK with those voices calling for new legislation to resolve the challenges of regulation it had identified. This enabled UUK to take a lead in informing a legislative process with potentially far-reaching implications for the sector. However, the need for legislation was not universally supported amongst UUK's membership owing to the risks of what might come through with it. There was common agreement that priorities needed to include protecting institutional autonomy and sector diversity, but less so on the best way to secure these, and the debate largely centred on the merits of a "fudge" versus clarity. A key challenge for UUK was, therefore, aligning members around a common set of priorities as well as the means of achieving these. The Gaskell report helped to reflect and coalesce membership and wider sector views around the need for legislation. On balance, the membership felt that the risks of no legislation were as high, if not higher, than the risk of new legislation. The Gaskell report also highlighted the view that new legislation was a means to achieving good outcomes rather than an end in itself. This approach de-emphasised the legislation-or-no-legislation question within UUK and meant that privately UUK could engage meaningfully with discussions already taking place in BIS[2] about what new legislation could look like. This would have been harder had UUK taken a stance to oppose legislation outright at that time.

The change in government and minister proved to be a key factor in new legislation being proposed. However, the Gaskell work meant that UUK was well prepared and already actively participating in discussions with government and beyond when the initial Green Paper was published. In addition, UUK was able to build on the broad principles established by Gaskell to work on new issues that emerged from the Green Paper. Equally, it was still necessary to establish and refine general principles, arguments, and specific proposals that could form a constructive but critical approach to the proposed legislation. These positions were established through a programme of engagement and consultation through UUK's policy networks and member meetings. These forums surfaced a series of themes in relation to the new legislation, including sector ownership of quality and standards and ensuring the new regulator was an arm's-length body. New areas in the Green Paper, such as the creation of the Teaching Excellence Framework (TEF, which became the Teaching Excellence and Student Outcomes Framework) and proposals for research funding emerging from Paul Nurse's review also presented complex challenges, not least because they would have varying impact across the different parts of the sector (Table 8.1).

Table 8.1 The ideas, strategy, and tactics during the process

Arguments	
World class reputation of the sector	The need for effective regulation that protects the sector's reputation founded on a high-quality educational experience for students.
Institutional autonomy	The need to ensure that universities of all types were free from directive and restrictive government intervention.
Co-regulation	The importance of ensuring that the sector itself, in particular that universities as autonomous bodies, had a stake in effective regulation.
Trade-offs	
Constructive partner for effective legislation	A careful balance between supporting passage of legislation while providing challenge to proposals.
Issue mobilisation and resource	Mobilising interest in technical detail while supporting parliamentarians in areas of interest.
Detail versus flexibility	Ensuring constraint on government powers while ensuring they were sufficiently flexible to future challenges.

Ideas, strategy, and tactics

This section examines UUK's strategy, tactics, and arguments throughout the process. UUK is an archetypal "insider" advocacy group in that it has well-established connections and relationships with civil servants and political parties. At the same time this position presented a dual risk of being simultaneously too close to government and insufficiently critical of proposals, as well as being a vested interest that was acting to prevent reform to the benefit of students. This required a careful calibration of arguments and a husbanding of political capital with an emphasis on the public interest in promoting a world-class, high-quality sector. UUK members and the UUK policy and communications teams had been involved in discussions about the need for reform since 2014 and were established as a credible voice with civil servants and ministers in this space. In the case of the Bill, this was aided by UUK's parliamentary presence, including links with the opposition that the Conservative Government did not have. The UUK membership itself was also crucial in this respect through their direct links to key parliamentarians and government ministers, often through their constituency roles.

In many respects the Lords, rather than the Commons, was the priority for UUK's parliamentary work. While there was a small but disciplined Conservative majority in the Commons, the Government was in the minority in the Lords. Furthermore, many members of the Lords had direct connections with universities and actively scrutinised the Bill throughout its passage. The Lords tend to be more independently minded and also have weaker party ties. As a result, many were receptive to UUK briefings and steers on the challenges presented by the Bill. At the same time, there was a dual risk in relation to UUK's positioning around the Bill and the different audiences that UUK engaged with during the process. The first risk was to be viewed, by both sides of the House, as a protectionist vested interest that was opposed to new entrants or any form of change in the system. The second risk was to be positioned too closely to government and lose the confidence of UUK's membership and parliament as an independent authoritative voice that could defend the sector's legitimate interests and challenge government proposals.

To navigate this challenge, UUK's arguments and strategy focused on the shared public interest of advancing the reputation and quality of a world-class sector. This meant acknowledging some of the basic tenets of the Government's policy agenda, particularly in relation to opening up the market to new entrants but ensuring that changes were contingent on securing the sector's reputation by maintaining high-quality thresholds. Managing these risks was also aided by a general recognition of the priority UUK placed on protecting the fundamental need for universities to be free from state interference. This was a principle that was shared by the Government's interest in market competition and the Lords who wanted to place appropriate constraint on government power over universities.

The idea of co-regulation was also helpful for bringing UUK's arguments and positioning together. Co-regulation is where stakeholder groups (in this case providers) and consumers (students) form part of the institutional setting for regulation. The concept has long been an implicit element of the Hefce approach (at least in terms of co-regulating with providers) and had been highlighted by the Gaskell report. It provided an organising rationale for ongoing engagement around the Bill and for carving out a stake for the sector in the new system. It also meant that provider and consumer interests aligned on key issues, given the enhanced stake that consumers potentially had in the new approaches being proposed. Co-regulation can be traced through elements in the final Act, such as the designated quality body and the protections around sector definition of standards.

One of the difficulties when seeking to formulate arguments about the detail of the Act was getting clear positions that had traction with parliamentarians and with civil servants and ministers. The HE sector's culture of nuance and consensus does not always play so well in the party politics of the Commons or the media. As a result, much of UUK's activity focused on private briefings, including private meetings and supporting issues papers, rather than more public media work or political campaigning. The first channel was direct engagement with government, often via civil servants rather than ministers, to examine specific and often technical issues in the Bill. The second channel focused on briefings to parliamentarians on specific issues of concern to help inform their scrutiny of the Bill.

In both cases, engagement on the Bill and specific issues of concern were supported by regular written and oral briefings that set out the principles and detail of concerns and potential ways forward. In all cases these briefings received an audience due to UUK's established position as an authoritative representative group and relationships. These briefings were shared with other groups or organisations that were also active in the process that helped to informally coordinate positions on the Bill and in some cases were supported by public outputs such as articles or blogs to help frame the arguments. The strength of these briefings came from seeking to constructively support government and parliament to examine potentially problematic areas and identify potential ways forward. At the same time, briefings sought to align UUK priorities and to distil technical issues in ways that engaged with the priorities of government and political stakeholders.

One notable area of scrutiny was TEF which, while a very small part of the Bill, attracted significant parliamentary attention. It generated significant scrutiny in the Commons due to the link with fees[3] and in the Lords due to the impact on institutional reputation. In addition, as a novel element of the regulatory framework that would rank universities, and a Conservative manifesto commitment, it had a profile in the sector and mainstream media. This interest in TEF risked crowding out some of the more detailed, albeit somewhat dry, nuances of sector architecture and autonomy. Nevertheless, UUK provided extensive briefings for parliamentarians to aid their scrutiny of TEF, alongside some gentle resistance to a role for parliament in the detail of its design.

The final trade-off related to the amount of detail that should be included in the Act and how it would be implemented. One of the mantras when thinking about legislation was not what the current government would do with the powers but what a future government might do with them, especially as the legislation establishing Hefce lasted 25 years.[4] More practically, this led to a careful balance between clearly specifying detailed powers that could establish a clear intent and associated constraints on their interpretation and use while providing a broad framework with enough flexibility to deal with the future. These arguments also tended to go back and forth with government depending on what either side was trying to secure, although UUK in the main sought greater specification to constrain government or OfS powers. However, UUK also sought to avoid inclusion of a detailed definition of a university in the Act and detail of the design of TEF in the Act as unhelpfully restrictive.

Decisions and outcomes

This section looks at some of the outcomes in the Act and UUK's own successes and limitations. While "success has many parents", UUK helped to secure approximately 30 significant amendments. Many of these tightened powers or introduced checks and balances or other forms of accountability, or established sector input into the new architecture through processes such as the designated data and quality bodies. At the same time, the Act leaves the sector with a regulator with significantly expanded powers to intervene, including powers of entry and exit into the market, new powers in relation to academic standards, as well as quality, and powerful performance tools such as TEF at its disposal. A non-exhaustive list of areas UUK worked on is sketched out in Table 8.2 by way of illustration.

There was a lot of parliamentary focus on the general statutory duties of OfS. UUK tended to support a broader approach that would leave space for flexibility and evolution but did support specific protections for institutional autonomy. In addition, it also worked to secure the inclusion of collaboration alongside competition as OfS general duties, to address concerns that this might undermine the benefits of a collegiate sector to students. However, UUK did not support including a definition of a university, given the risks

Table 8.2 Decisions and outcomes

Internal UUK score card

Statutory duties	Secured the inclusion of collaboration alongside competition in the general statutory duties of OfS. Secured protection for institutional autonomy in the act.
Quality and standards	Failed to get standards out of the act – a Government red line – but did secure changes to the Bill to ensure that quality and standards were properly defined, protection for institutional academic autonomy, and sector ownership of the definition of standards for purposes of regulation. Worked with civil servants on designated bodies approach.
DAPs and validation	Tightened regulation around degree awarding powers and university title, including the creation of a strong, independent body to scrutinise DAPs and UT. Failed to prevent OfS validation powers but did secure ministerial oversight of the powers. Did not support defining a university. Protections were secured for royal chartered universities.
Search and entry	Failed to get substantial movement on this as a tool for OfS.
TEF	Avoided additional detail in relation to the design of TEF. Secured introduction of a legislative requirement for an independent review of TEF beginning in 2018, and a delay in the introduction of subject-level TEF by a year, with an additional pilot year.
Immigration amendment	Gave support but did not make it a priority pending alternative policy avenues and potentially shifting political support in favour of it at the time.
Essay mills[a]	Gave support to the Lord Storey proposals to make it an offence to provide services, but interest in government did not fully materialise to take it forward due to Ministry of Justice opposition to introducing new law without more evidence of need and potential impact.
UKRI	A new requirement for annual reporting of how UK Research and Innovation and OfS cooperate, and an amendment to embed the Haldane Principle (that decisions on where to spend research funds should be taken by researchers) on the face of the Bill with respect to allocation of funds by UKRI.

---

[a] Essay mills provide services in the form of bespoke essays that are sold to students with the explicit or implicit suggestion that they can be fraudulently submitted to secure required grades. The Quality Assurance Agency for Higher Education has been active in identifying ways to combat these services.

of entrenching an inflexible proscriptive model set by parliament. The inclusion of standards was a significant expansion of scope for OfS in comparison to Hefce and the 1992 Act which raised a potential risk to UUK members' academic discretion over curricula and assessment. However, the inclusion of standards was a red line for the Government, as illustrated by a photo in the *Telegraph* of briefing notes on the way in to No.10 Downing Street.

UUK worked with civil servants to redraft the definition of standards to require them to be recognised by the sector, preventing OfS from mandating its own and limiting the scope for future governments to push toward standardised curricula.

UUK was active in relation to market entry, with a focus on checks and balances in the process for granting degree awarding powers. UUK failed to get movement in areas such as temporary degree-awarding powers, given the centrality to the Government's agenda of encouraging new entrants and market competition. Neither did UUK prevent the inclusion of the power for OfS to act as a "validator of last resort". UUK opposed this on principled and practical grounds as it meant that a government body would effectively be granting itself degree-awarding powers with no academic competency, and creating conflicts in associated regulation and assessment of quality. Again, the fall-back position was on appropriate accountability, including Secretary of State approval, and commitments in the House about how the powers were intended to be used.

Parliamentary interest in TEF was probably well-justified, given the likely prominence of the scheme in the long run. UUK gently opposed entrenching parliamentary input into the detailed design of TEF due to the risk it would restrict future changes and space for the sector to exert influence over its design. At the same time, UUK supported parliamentary scrutiny of TEF and the interest, and opposition, in the Lords ultimately helped to secure the independent review.[5] Government needed to make concessions to the Lords for the Bill to pass before the dissolution of parliament for the 2017 General Election, despite the fact that TEF was a 2015 manifesto commitment which, by convention, the Lords tend not to oppose.

When assessing UUK's influence on the strategic policy agenda, the picture is perhaps less clear. UUK successfully promoted, with caveats, protections for autonomy and elements of co-regulation in the new system. These elements will be important, as the Act gives OfS a comprehensive set of powers, alongside an agenda of bringing new providers into the system. How these powers evolve into an effective regulatory framework will depend on how the Act is interpreted and implemented, which is still ongoing. In this respect, principles such as co-regulation give the sector a stake in this process. UUK also failed to secure inclusion of a broader concern in the health of institutions themselves. This opens risks that OfS may view the relationship between institutions and students as a transactional or adversarial one when using its new powers. Ultimately, this will be down to how OfS interprets its agenda within the framework of powers and checks and balances established by the Act. The outcomes of the review of post-18 education funding, initiated in 2018, will likely test how "future proofed" the Act is and the durability of OfS's envisaged role as a regulator rather than a funding body.

Conclusion

This quick tour down memory lane illustrates how policy work upstream by external bodies can directly and indirectly shape the landscape for decisions years down the line. Indeed, questions such as preventing and managing institutional failure were present in the post-2012 discussion and remain live debates. The account presented here is by no means comprehensive but shows how engaging with tangible problems and short-term fixes presents opportunities to set the longer-term agenda for change. One of the biggest challenges for interest groups, particularly membership organisations, in realising the opportunities for influencing policy upstream and beyond is being able to cohere membership around the need for action. The early work enabled UUK to have clear positions on the important issues and prepared the ground for it to be able to engage in the significant debates ahead on the future of sector regulation. This is not to say that other influences and actors were not active (for example, see the Higher Education Commission 2013) but, as a significant player, UUK had a clear voice and platform. It also enabled ideas to be discussed and "socialised" with those officials within government and Hefce who were preparing thinking, should an opportunity for legislation arise.

The process of engaging with the Act itself can be understood as a constructive negotiation with government, both directly and through parliament. UUK's approach in this process had to strike the right balance between views within the membership and in relation to government as a critical friend. From UUK's perspective, the negotiation with government centred on the shared recognition of the need to update legislation and a common interest in promoting a high-quality sector. From here, the Government wanted more power to advance the student interest and to encourage competition. UUK wanted to protect institutional autonomy, including a sector stake in defining entry and quality and standards. However, while UUK had authority in the debate it has no direct decision-making power in the policymaking or legislative process. This position necessitates using political capital with those that do, carefully and wisely.

UUK's successes came, to a significant degree, from being seen as an authoritative source of expertise due to the breadth and depth of its membership, its political networks, and policy work. Again, this entailed carefully balancing member views and the organisation's policy and political positioning to maintain this authority. The success of this alignment was predicated on a shared recognition of the importance of an autonomous and diverse sector in parliament and government, a persistent strategic priority for UUK that was achieved both before and through the legislative process. To maintain and develop this position UUK worked to understand the respective aims and interests of government and parliament to identify where there was common ground that would enable proposals to be refined and to land them effectively. Being a trusted source of advice and support in the Lords helped to support scrutiny of the Act beyond UUK's priorities as well.

UUK exerted practical and political influence throughout the process but was more constrained in relation to the fundamentals of the Government's agenda. This was rooted in the trade-off in the value of being a critical friend versus being an outright opponent, and the respective limits of both positions. In the case of the Higher Education and Research Act 2017 government had a democratic mandate and set out its reform agenda through the White and Green Papers. As a result, the focus quickly became how to ensure the Bill produced an effective framework, while promoting UUK's strategic priorities, such as autonomy. Organisations such as UUK can influence the options presented to ministers and parliament but the terms of the debate are largely set at a political level through a government's electoral and parliamentary mandate. An organisation such as UUK can, and perhaps should, be active in seeking to set the terms of the political debate. But it must also be mindful of the risks of being viewed as overly political and self-interested that can have consequences for the credibility and authority of the organisation and its avenues of influence over time.

Ultimately, UUK engaged with the Act to update the statutory underpinnings of sector regulation while seeking to protect against a significant and unnecessary extension of government powers. OfS is a powerful new regulator with a broad mandate to focus on the interests of students rather than the interests of providers themselves. In practice the interests of students and their universities should align but this shift still represents a significant departure from the previous Hefce model. The priority now for many universities and the sector more generally is to establish a mature relationship with OfS. At the same time OfS is seeking to establish itself as an active and independent player in the HE policy and regulatory landscape that is willing to take action where necessary. By engaging constructively with the legislative process and the wider reform agenda, UUK was able to shape the policy agenda while securing important clarifications to OfS's mission and checks and balances on its powers. In this respect the Act hopefully provides the foundations for effective regulation of HE that helps to ensure students receive a high-quality education, and with it secures the wider social and economic benefits of HE.

Notes

1 The Higher Education and Research Act is primarily concerned with regulation of higher education in England through the establishment of the Office for Students; the reorganisation of the research councils and the formation of UK Research Innovation was a UK-wide matter.

2 There was a machinery of government change following the 2016 referendum that moved competency for the teaching aspect of HE from the Department for Business, Innovation and Skills into the Department for Education. The research element remained in the remodelled Department for Business, Energy and Industrial Strategy. This change reflected the proposed delineation between teaching and research funding outlined in the 2016 White Paper and subsequently established by the HERA.

3 The Secretary of State retains the power through the HERA to link fees caps to performance in TEF, including setting a sub-level amount between the £9,000 cap and an upper cap that is limited by inflation. However, government shifted policy following the 2017 General Election and froze the upper cap at £9,250 pending the post-18 education funding review.

4 Notably the provisions in the 1992 Act relating to Hefce and higher education institutions were relatively short in comparison to HERA, approximately 30 pages plus schedules, and focused largely on the distribution of funding and the granting of the title of university to the former polytechnics, a short section requiring Hefce to make arrangements to assess the quality of provision that it funded, and powers, such as efficiency studies and information provision, that reappeared in HERA in amended forms.

5 The independent review of TEF was carried out by Dame Shirley Pearce in early 2019 and was due to be published in summer 2019.

References

BIS (2011) *Higher Education White Paper – Students at the Heart of the System.* London: Department for Business, Innovation and Skills. Available from: www.gov.uk/government/consultations/higher-education-white-paper-students-at-the-heart-of-the-system

Hammonds, W (2018) *Policy-Making, Paradigms and Change: The Origins of the Prevent Counter Terrorism Policy in Great Britain Between 2001 and 2011.* Colchester: University of Essex. Available from: repository.essex.ac.uk/23317/

Hefce (2015a) *Regulatory Partnership Group.* Bristol: Higher Education Funding Council for England. Available from: webarchive.nationalarchives.gov.uk/20180319123209/http://www.hefce.ac.uk/about/unicoll/other/RPG/

Hefce (2015b) *Agreement on Institutional Designation.* Bristol: Higher Education Funding Council for England. Available from: webarchive.nationalarchives.gov.uk/20180319122033/http://www.hefce.ac.uk/reg/agreement/

Hefce (2017) *Memorandum of Assurance and Accountability.* Bristol: Higher Education Funding Council for England. Available from: webarchive.nationalarchives.gov.uk/20180319120008/http://www.hefce.ac.uk/reg/MAA/

Higher Education Commission (2013) *Regulating Higher Education.* London: Policy Connect. Available from: www.policyconnect.org.uk/hec/research/report-regulating-higher-education

Nurse, P (2015) *Ensuring a Successful UK Research Endeavour: A Review of the UK Research Councils*. London: Department for Business, Innovation and Skills.

UUK (2015) *Quality, Equity, Sustainability: The Future of Higher Education Regulation*. London: Universities UK. Available from: www.universitiesuk.ac.uk/policy-and-analysis/reports/Documents/2015/quality-equity-sustainability.pdf

CHAPTER 9

Delivering Diamond

A policy development case study of student funding in Wales

Dewi Knight

Introduction

On the face of it, it wasn't the easiest of cards to be dealt. The only Liberal Democrat member of the Senedd (Welsh Parliament) and the sole non-Labour Minister in the Cabinet, with a full house of education reforms to pursue but having to declare a new policy on tuition fees and student finance.

But there was an ace in the hole. A diamond. A chance, not without risk, to go all-in on delivering a unique, progressive, and sustainable finance and support system for all Welsh students and universities.

In this chapter, I will look at the who, what, why, and when of moving forward with Professor Sir Ian Diamond's 2016 *Review of Higher Education Funding and Student Finance Arrangements*, supporting a minister in making the argument for change, and building a consensus for implementation. I will focus on the importance of establishing and articulating a set of principles. Many who are engaged in higher education (HE) policy and public affairs are used to the expediency of change. The success of system reform in Wales, I suggest, owes a great deal to framing the case for change around guiding principles which bridged politics and policy.

As the Institute for Government reported in 2011, "[c]ivil servants generally see the ideal minister as one who can set principles and articulate goals, but then is willing to listen to official advice on how to realize their aims through evidence, analysis and recommendations" (Hallsworth, Parker, and Rutter 2011, 95). As a specialist adviser in government, my telling of this story is shaped by the experience of working closely with some of the best civil servants in Welsh Government, with an Education Minister prepared to make the big calls and "lead from the front", and with student and sector leaders willing to have the necessary honest and frank conversations. These will, of course, be my perspective and reflections. Others will reflect on different key moments, have learned different lessons, made different connections. But I hope it proves an informative, and interesting, report on what it takes to turn principles into policy.

Context

27 September 2016 was "Diamond Day". That's how it was it was described in the ministerial diary, in the Government's announcements "grid", and as shorthand in the sector for the day that the report would be published. But, for me and the government team working round the clock on the details of potential changes in student support, led superbly by civil servants Neil Surman and Chris Jones, there were plenty of other Diamond Days, perhaps even Diamond weeks. The review of Wales's HE funding and finance was commissioned by the then Education Minister (Huw Lewis, Labour Assembly Member for Merthyr Tydfil and Rhymney) back in late 2013 (Lewis 2014). Welsh post-16 education has been well served by reviews chaired by leading international figures, much of this down to the broad horizons of another Huw (Morris, Director of Skills, HE and Lifelong Learning, Welsh Government). As with the Browne Review in England (2010), the report would be presented to the next Government; in this case, in September 2016, after the Welsh General Election in May that year. The review panel, led by Diamond, included heads of universities in Wales, funding experts such as Dr Gavan Conlon from London Economics, the President of NUS Wales, and representatives from the (then) opposition political parties.

The terms of reference included "conduct[ing] a wide-ranging review of HE sector funding and student finance arrangements" (Lewis 2014). However, it was evident that the sustainability of the then Welsh Government's policy of paying a tuition fee grant (worth c. £5,000) for full-time undergraduates, and the opportunity cost of this for other student support and wider HE investment, would be the main conundrum to solve. There had been increasing noise around that policy, led in particular by Welsh vice-chancellors. This culminated in a Universities Wales (2015) policy statement, recommending "discontinuing a universal tuition fee grant which only supports full-time undergraduate students", to allow "better targeting towards those that need it most, ... [and] funding higher education policies which equip our universities to deliver economic growth ... [and] a high quality offering for students studying via all types of modes".

The review timetable, running from 2014 through to late summer 2016, took the immediate political pressure away. However, the party election manifestos published in spring 2016 showed that there was yet to be a consensus on next steps for student and higher education finance. Welsh Labour (2016) committed to a "better package of student support than that on offer in England, based on the recommendations of the Diamond Review". Plaid Cymru (2016) offered to pay Welsh graduates who worked in Wales "£6,000 per year during the first five years after graduating, up to a maximum of £18,000", and although they didn't mention maintenance grants, they did promise loans for post-graduates. The Welsh Liberal Democrat (2016) manifesto pledged to abolish the tuition fee grant and introduce a "Student Living Support Grant" for all Welsh domiciled students. In a surprise move, Huw Lewis announced in early 2016 that he would stand down as an Assembly Member (AM) at the election. So there would definitely be a new Minister responsible for responding to Diamond, but the eventual occupant of the hotseat will have been a surprise to many.

Progressive agreement

Kirsty Williams, the Liberal Democrat AM for Brecon and Radnorshire, become Wales's Education Minister on 19 May 2016. Following the election that month, Welsh Labour was once again returned as comfortably the largest party but short of a majority. In the days that followed the election, which had left Kirsty as the only remaining Liberal Democrat (from a group of five in the previous parliament), she and (then) First Minister Carwyn Jones negotiated an agreement on a set of education (and other) priorities. Despite spending years leading the charge to the First Minister during questions in the Senedd and in leaders' debates during the campaign, Williams and Jones had a good relationship: they had both been elected in the first devolution elections of 1999, and worked closely together as the business managers for the respective parliamentary groups in those early days of the new parliament. Of a similar age, their centre-left instincts are not dissimilar, and having chosen to pursue their political careers in Cardiff Bay rather than Westminster, their rise to leadership positions had long been predicted.

Over a period of three days in the week following the election, Williams shuttled between her office on the third floor of Ty Hywel (the parliamentary building that houses AMs' offices) and the First Minister's office on the fifth floor (the floor for ministerial private offices). The good relationship, and ease at finding common ground, meant that the "progressive agreement" went through fewer than ten iterations. On student finance, the agreed wording was that "[t]he recommendations of the Diamond Review are considered, with a view to early implementation where appropriate, but there will be no negative effect on the higher education budget if there are any changes" (Welsh Government 2016b). An earlier draft of the agreement included the line "prioritising support for student living costs"; however, it was sensibly agreed that, as this was expected to be the main focus of the report, it didn't need to be highlighted in such a way.

In recalling the First Minister's offer, Williams remembers that he lightheartedly referred to those Senedd question-time sessions by saying "you always bang on about education, let's see what you can do". But recognising that changes in student finance might be politically challenging, it was briefly mooted that Williams would have the option of allowing a Deputy Minister to lead on the issue. This was quickly dismissed out of hand as she was confident that the progressive agreement was a matter of good principle and good policy and had no interest in ducking the challenge. The various contortions of Lib Dem MPs and Ministers in Westminster around the issue had shown that any such abdication wouldn't wash with the public.

Guiding principles

I joined the Government in August 2016 as a specialist policy adviser, but in the weeks from May had informally being doing preparatory work on Williams's reform programme, including student finance. We learned from the Coalition's difficulties in England that there was a fundamental need to frame the task at hand and provide a recognisably new starting point for responding to the report. Williams (2016d) has described this as being "able to balance – and to blend – principles and practicalities". Williams gave her first keynote speech as a Minister on 8 September 2016 at Cardiff University's Business School. By this time Diamond had submitted his final report to the Minister, allowing her to take it to Cabinet before publication later that month. Ironically, the venue for the speech was now the home turf for one of her predecessors as Education Minister, (the now) Professor Leighton Andrews, who had introduced the funding regime under review from Diamond.

In the speech, Williams challenged the sector to recapture a sense of civic mission. However, we were acutely aware that any talk of community stewardship, civic purpose, and the university in the public square, would only have the ear of the audience if we also addressed the forthcoming Diamond Report and wider issues of higher education finance. Having referenced Raymond Williams, American land grant colleges, and the Aberdare Committee of 1881, Williams came to the issue of student and higher education finance. She said:

> Sir Ian and his cross-party panel of experts have been diligent in their work. I am hopeful that we can be optimistic, ambitious and innovative in bringing forward a settlement that: maintains the principle of universalism within a progressive system; for the first time anywhere in the UK, ensures a fair and consistent approach across levels and modes of study; ensures shared investment between government and those who directly benefit; and enhances accessibility, reducing barriers to study such as living costs.
>
> (Williams 2016a)

These – and the commitment "that student support is portable across the UK" – had at the same time been put on the front page of a paper that was going to the Welsh Government Cabinet for a meeting the following week. In that paper, which provided Cabinet with the Diamond Report and recommended the policy and financial way forward, Williams sought support to "welcome the strategic direction" of the report, and described the five points as her "guiding principles for a sustainable student finance system and the Welsh Government response". This followed Cabinet agreement (in July) for the progressive agreement commitment (in slightly revised language): "confirm[ing] that it is Welsh Government's intention to implement any Welsh Government response to the recommendations as a single package of reforms as soon as is practicable with no negative effect on the higher education budget" (Welsh Government 2016a).

With the First Minister's full backing, September's Cabinet unanimously approved the Government's response and the principles for reform. The principles were also framed as tests for the new settlement, as civil servants continued work on modelling a new package, in line with the Government's proposed response (I detail below the slight modifications between the Government's policy and Diamond's report). These principles (or tests) were informed by the review panel's work. But they were also an iteration of the Liberal Democrat manifesto commitment, and in line with Labour's pledge on securing a better deal for Welsh students. It doesn't need extended retelling here that this was rather different from the situation in Westminster in 2010. And as David Willetts (2017) has pointed out, Lib Dem candidates signed the famous pledge to abolish fees "despite several members, such as Vince Cable and David Laws, recognising that this was unaffordable". To my mind, it is this cynicism, and failure to link principles and policy, which is the main political and policy lesson from that period. And it is one that Williams was determined to avoid.

Having cross-party representation on the panel was an advantage. But this did not tie the party spokespeople and leaders to supporting the report or government response. And although Williams's principles were not universally supported across the political and policy spectrum – portability and the universal element being the main areas of disagreement – they were in line with the report.

Hearts and minds

The build-up to the publication day was an exciting, if challenging, period. This was two weeks on from Cabinet agreement in mid-September. We couldn't be completely confident of the reaction and needed to work closely with key stakeholders in finding the sweet spot of managing expectations whilst also underlining the appetite for radical changes. Of course, the main challenge was being careful about what could be shared with those external stakeholders. This is where the agreed principles were crucial to the story we were telling, but also in ensuring an understanding of how the report might land. Those who paid close attention would have been able to read between the lines. An appreciation of Williams's ability as a political operator should have led to an implicit understanding. She would not have set those principles and tests without being confident of the government's direction of travel in meeting them. In those two weeks between Cabinet and publication of the report, government backbenchers, vice-chancellors, leaders of national HE organisations (in Wales and UK-wide), and members of the review panel all received face-to-face or telephone briefings (from myself, Neil Surman, or Williams's political adviser Tom Woodward, depending on the context of the relationship).

The script for these calls and briefings, and a briefing note that was made available to selected stakeholders, was boiled down to one page. We were careful not to say more – or less – than appeared on that one-pager. There was not only a necessity of not breaking confidences or the pre-publication embargo, but brevity also afforded a real focus. I would always recommend such an approach ahead of any similar process. Indeed, it is now a discipline we follow for any major policy announcement, including a new national schools' strategy, reducing class sizes, or eligibility for free school meals. Those government "guiding principles" were right at the top of the briefing. This allowed us to be consistent, but also to successfully frame those conversations. As with any policy implementation, principles have to sit alongside practicalities. The Diamond Review Panel itself set out its own 16 "guiding principles" for a "funding strategy" in HE (Diamond 2016). These take a broader view and include references to academic freedom and economic contexts.

For telling a story of reform and for framing a decision, only three to five principles can be truly effective. It allows for constructive repetition, it provides a better focus, and it allows you to draw a direct line between the principles and policy delivery. The first principle on "universalism" was met by the guarantee that all students, no matter their household income, would receive an element of the support as a non-repayable grant. Our second principle on the "whole system" approach, across mode and level of study, is being delivered through the equivalent support package, in grant and loan, for full- and part-time undergraduates as well as master's students. The third principle of shared investment between government and those who directly benefit is addressed by maintaining the graduate contribution (through income-contingent repayment of fee loans) while focusing investment on generous upfront grants for living costs. The fourth, to enhance accessibility and address living costs, is met by the commitment on part-time and post-graduate support, while also ensuring that the support is particularly generous for those from lower-income households and that care leavers get the full grant package. And finally, the fifth principle of portability was delivered by ensuring that the funding follows the students wherever they choose to study in the UK.

A system that provides for all

Neil Surman and I spoke to all Welsh vice-chancellors and heads of HE organisations the day before both the publication of the report and the Ministerial statement. We had to clear a whole day to get through these calls. Still being relatively new in post it was a good window onto the effectiveness of vice-chancellors' lobbying. Some, such as Cardiff University, Swansea University, and the University of South Wales had questions ready and were astute enough to raise other issues (Professor Colin Riordan, Cardiff's vice-chancellor, had been a member of the review panel and, alongside fellow member Rob Humphreys, Director of The Open University in Wales, had done much to prepare the ground with their fellow leaders). Others, oddly, were happy with receiving the five-minute script and getting on with other business. The inconsistency and ineffectiveness of much HE public affairs and civic engagement continue to baffle me. Although we could not directly brief those vice-chancellors and executives on current Government thinking on the response, it was clear that many of them had been able to read between the lines on the principles and what that likely meant for implementation.

Perhaps the most famous principles regarding higher education reform, in the UK at least, are presented in the Robbins Report (1963). In fact, the most prominent of these principles – that "higher education should be available for all those who are qualified by ability" – was referenced by Diamond in the foreword to his report. In her statement to the Senedd on the day of the Diamond Report publication, Williams welcomed that "the Panel's work was guided by the long-standing Robbins principle that entry into higher education should be on the basis of ability alone, not on the ability to afford it". Although the statement did not set out the full details of the Government's response, the Education Minister set out that Cabinet had "endorsed the underlying principles contained in the report [and] now needs to consider the practical implications of implementing its recommendations" (Williams 2016b). During the statement, she drew a direct line between this, the report, and her own principles for the government's response (at the time, subject to agreement with the Student Loans Company (SLC) and the UK Treasury). After setting out the five principles during the statement, first referenced in her civic mission speech at Cardiff University and then through the cabinet paper, Williams concluded her statement by once again referencing the Robbins principles – but highlighting a different one. She said:

> In my agreement with the First Minister, we recognised that "high quality education is the driving force for social mobility, national prosperity and an engaged democracy". To enable this, Wales needs a sustainable and progressive higher education funding settlement that supports students when they most need it, and enables our universities to compete internationally. I started by referring to the famous principle of the Robbins report. It is often overlooked that in setting out the aims of a higher education system, the report also said that "The system as a whole must be judged deficient unless it provides adequately for all". Sir Ian and his panel have today brought forward a report that recommends a fundamental shift so that Wales can develop a higher education funding and student finance system that really does provide for all.

The abiding image of the day was the photo used by many media outlets – that of Diamond, the Education Minister and Fflur Elin, then NUS Wales President, standing together in support of the published report.

Conclusion

Within two months, Williams was back in the Senedd to present the Government's full response to the report's recommendations. Much of the background work that took place in September was repeated ahead of the November publication. The one-pager was updated, but still with the Cabinet-endorsed principles at its heart, and we were able to provide information on our modelling for government backbenchers and opposition spokespeople. Once again, a day was cleared for meetings and phone calls with key stakeholders, but this time with more details on our timetable for proposed implementation. The Minister's statement was drafted with an explicit link between the principles and the policy package she was taking forward. In that statement, Williams (2016c) was able to "confirm that we are implementing, with only minor modification, the full Diamond Package, whilst also delivering a future dividend for further and higher education. This, of course, would be subject to normal government budget negotiation and process". The term "minor modification" was carefully chosen to reflect the slight changes between selected Diamond recommendations and Government policy, but in line with the guiding principles. These modifications were limited but included a lower increase (than proposed in the report) to the upper threshold of household income for means-tested support (so that it was set at £59,200) and extending ELQ (equivalent or lower qualifications) exemptions rather than abolishing them completely. However, Williams made it clear that the fundamental next step for Wales's student finance system was:

> to deliver the first system in the UK – and be an international model of best practice – that is consistent, progressive and fair in its support for full and part-time undergraduates and for post-graduate students. Our response recognises the consensus that it is the fear of not being able to meet daily living costs, rather than the prospect of paying back loans once in work, that is the bigger issue for accessing and progressing through higher education.

Delivering that radical new system, in time for the 2018/19 academic year, was a tremendous collective effort from the Welsh Government's higher education division, the Student Loans Company, the Higher Education Funding Council for Wales (Hefcw), and others.

The grant and loans support for part-time undergraduates and post-graduates – "the whole system" principle – is arguably the most radical element, and with potentially the biggest individual and economic impact. At the time of writing in early 2019, projections show a double-figure percentage increase in part-time undergraduates and master's students. This of course is in stark contrast to England's reforms, which led to David Willetts (2017) saying that "one of my biggest regrets in office is that we presided over a big fall in numbers of part-time students". Of course, just having principles doesn't necessarily make for good policy. Government, policymaking, independent reviews, coalition building, and political handling are a sophisticated and, at times, messy business. However, they provide the firm ground upon which policy can grow. And just as importantly they provide an ongoing benchmark for the success, and necessary challenge, for policy delivery.

To refer back to the Institute for Government report, the Education Minister was able to set clear principles and goals, and win support for these in government, politically and within the sector. It is from these that we were able to deliver on Diamond's recommendations, realising those principles through sound advice and evidence. That is the full house of turning principles into policy and delivering far-reaching education reforms.

References

Browne, J (2010) *Securing a Sustainable Future for Higher Education: An Independent Review of Higher Education Funding & Student Finance*. London: Department for Business, Innovation and Skills.

Diamond, I (2016) *The Review of Higher Education Funding and Student Finance Arrangements in Wales*. Cardiff: Welsh Government Offices. Available from:

beta.gov.wales/sites/default/files/publications/2018-02/higher-education-funding-final-report-en.pdf

Hallsworth, M with S Parker and J Rutter (2011) *Policy Making in the Real World*. London: Institute for Government. Available from: www.instituteforgovernment.org.uk/sites/default/files/publications/Policy%20making%20in%20the%20real%20world.pdf

Lewis, H (2014, 19 February) *Written Statement – Statement on the Review of Higher Education Funding and Student Finance Arrangements in Wales*. Cardiff: Welsh Government Offices. Available from: gov.wales/about/cabinet/cabinetstatements/previous-administration/2014/hefinance/?lang=en

Plaid Cymru (2016) *The Change Wales Needs*. Cardiff: Plaid Cymru.

Robbins, LC (1963) *Higher Education: Report of the Committee*. London: HMSO.

Universities Wales (2015) *Delivering for Wales: The Higher Education Priorities for the Future Welsh Government*. Cardiff: Universities Wales. Available from: www.uniswales.ac.uk/media/Delivering-for-Wales-The-Higher-Education-Priorities-for-the-Future-Welsh-Government2.pdf

Welsh Government offices (2016a, 13 September) *Minutes of a Meeting of the Cabinet*. Cardiff: Welsh Government Offices. Available from: gov.wales/about/cabinet/meetings/2016-2021new/13september2016/?lang=en

Welsh Government offices (2016b, 23 June) *Working Together to Take Wales Forward*. Cardiff: Welsh Government Offices. Available from: gov.wales/newsroom/firstminister/2016/160623-working-together-to-take-wales-forward/?lang=en

Welsh Labour (2016) *Together for Wales*. Cardiff: Welsh Labour.

Welsh Liberal Democrats (2016) *A Wales that Works for You*. Cardiff: Welsh Liberal Democrats.

Willetts, D (2017) *A University Education*. Oxford: Oxford University Press.

Williams, K (2016a, 8 September) *The Brexit University Challenge: Recapturing a Civic Mission*. Cardiff: Welsh Government Offices. Available from: beta.gov.wales/brexit-university-challenge-recapturing-civic-mission

Williams, K (2016b, 27 September) *Oral Statement – The Diamond Review of Higher Education and Student Finance in Wales*. Cardiff: Welsh Government Offices. Available from: gov.wales/about/cabinet/cabinetstatements/2016-new/diamondreviewhe/?lang=en

Williams, K (2016c, 22 November) *Oral Statement – The Diamond Review of Higher Education and Student Finance in Wales*. Cardiff: National Assembly for Wales. Available from: assembly.wales/en/bus-home/pages/rop.aspx?meetingid=4006&assembly=5&c=Record%20of%20Proceedings#C441773

Williams, K (2016d, 7 December) *Principles and Practicalities*. Cardiff: Welsh Government Offices. Available from: beta.gov.wales/principles-and-practicalities

CHAPTER 10

Performance measurement and student information in the UK

Adapting to a diverging policy context between Scotland and England

Cathy Mitchell

Introduction

This chapter examines Scotland's position in the UK higher education (HE) sector, considering the increasing differences between each nation's system of HE, but also their shared history which ensures that each country's HE policy does not play out in isolation. The systemic divergence in HE policy since devolution is apparent in many areas, and these have been explored since the powers for HE policy were devolved to Scotland in 1999 (Bruce 2012). This chapter builds on this theme of divergence by adding the performance measurement and student information space as a new area where the HE policies of the two countries are growing apart as a result of the acceleration of the marketisation approach of English HE.

The performance measurement and student information space covers all data-based methods of rating the performance of an institution. There are many aspects of student information and performance measurement that are shared across the UK. The Higher Education Statistics Agency (HESA) and the Universities and Colleges Admissions Service (UCAS) are both UK-wide organisations providing data services in the UK context. There are annual UK-wide Performance Indicators (UKPIs) published for institutions, UK-wide league tables that handle data in the same way for all regions, and the National Student Survey (NSS) is run UK-wide. The four UK funding bodies also have a Memorandum of Understanding for the Provision of Information for Students detailing how collective and respective objectives are delivered, and student information is shared on the UK-wide Unistats website for students. From an applicant's point of view, HE is still a UK-wide market. This chapter looks at how substantial and sustainable this view is.

Performance measurement is used in Scotland as a way of ensuring institutions are operating to a high standard and that the Scottish Government receives a return on investment for the public spending allocated to universities. This is achieved through Outcome Agreements (OAs) in a process that is largely separate from student information. In England, where the design of the system assumes that it is primarily the student who requires a return on their investment, performance measurement and student information are increasingly one and the same thing. The data-driven and regulatory metrics in this area increasingly have prospective students as the target audience, tying them to the marketisation agenda, and this is putting Scotland's position in the UK performance measurement and student information space at risk. There is a need for greater scrutiny of how the distinction between sector performance measurement and student information is being blurred and also a need for a better understanding of the role that these shared metrics have in influencing and shaping HE policy across UK borders. This chapter also questions the role of data in HE policy, and also how each UK country develops policy in this area given how much is shared across the UK.

Diverging context

Scotland and England shared a similar path towards marketisation in the 1980s and 1990s, prior to devolution. The Education Reform Act 1988 and the Further and Higher Education Act 1992 transformed HE in both Scotland and England, coinciding with a peak of the marketisation surge in UK public utilities and services in 1994 (Williams 2004, 241). This direction of travel towards marketisation had led the UK, including Scotland, to being seen as closer to the US HE system than any of the European systems (Brown and Carasso 2013, 7).

Marketisation in the HE context is the value of education becoming understood in monetary terms, and is evident in developments such as the separation of teaching and research funding, the introduction and increases of tuition fees, the empowerment of students as consumers, and the relaxation of rules to allow new providers to enter the sector (Raffe and Croxford 2013, 3). These are features that are more recognisable in the English sector than in the Scottish sector, and overall there has been much less appetite for these market-based reforms in any of the devolved countries (Bruce 2012). This difference is frequently illustrated by the divergence in tuition fee policy. From the same starting point in 1998, the two countries are now far apart in their tuition fee policies, with Scotland offering free tuition to Scottish and EU domiciled undergraduate students, and English institutions charging their UK students as much as £9,250 for 2019 entry. Table 10.1 shows the timeline of steps that each country took in reaching their current positions.

As of 2019, fees for Scottish and non-UK students from the European Union are paid by the Scottish Government through the Student Awards Agency Scotland (SAAS), underlying the policy of "free tuition", whereas students from the rest of the UK (rUK) are eligible to pay for these supported by

Table 10.1 Scotland and England tuition fee timeline

	Scotland	England
1992	Separate HE funding councils created across the UK	
1998	Annual tuition fee of £1,000 introduced in the UK	
1999	Elements of HE policy devolved to Scotland, Wales, and Northern Ireland	
2000	Fee replaced in Scotland with a one-off £2,000 deferred graduate endowment	
2006	Fee raised to £1,700, affecting the rUK students eligible to pay	Annual tuition fee increased in England to £3,000
2007	Graduate endowment abolished in Scotland	
2012	Higher variable tuition fees introduced for rUK students, rUK students removed from the SFC funded place calculation	Annual tuition fee in England increased to £9,000
2015		Cap on student numbers removed in England
2018		Funding Council in England, Hefce, replaced by regulatory body, OfS

Figures shown at the amount they were introduced and do not show changes due to inflationary uplifts.

loans. The fees, whether they came from SAAS or from rUK students, are only part of the total cost of tuition: the remaining amount is paid by the Scottish Funding Council (SFC). Scotland's policy of tuition fees that are free at the point of delivery largely relies on the ethos of university education as a public good and of benefit to the greater society in justifying the public spend. The SFC OA guidance for academic year 2019–20 states that

> working in partnership with our institutions, [SFC] want the 317,000 students in our universities and colleges to have the best possible learning experience so that they are equipped to think, to act, and to contribute in their workplaces and in their communities within Scotland – and beyond.
>
> (SFC 2018b, 1)

The SFC Strategic Plan for 2015–19 further states that SFC's "task is to care for and develop the whole system of colleges and universities and their connections and contribution to Scotland's educational, social, cultural and economic life" (SFC 2015). This captures the idea of HE as a public, rather than individual, good and highlights students' contribution to society as one of the main benefits of university study. The continuing ethos in Scotland and in its regulatory framework is one of HE as a public good, in contrast with the growing marketisation that can be seen elsewhere in HE (Raffe and Croxford 2013, 6).

Another relevant area of difference is in the quality assurance of HE. In 1997, the Quality Assurance Agency for Higher Education (QAA) was created as a UK-wide independent body to ensure comparable quality and standards. However, QAA has a separate Scottish office and the Scottish sector has its own arrangements for quality. SFC itself has a statutory obligation to ensure that provision is made for assessing and enhancing the quality of fundable HE (SFC 2017). The approach to quality in Scotland is fundamentally different in ethos, with SFC taking a more progressive approach compared to the risk-based, regulatory-only approach taken by the Office for Students (OfS). The SFC Quality Enhancement Framework (QEF) guidance encourages collaboration between universities in Scotland (SFC 2017) and the framework builds upon the "extraordinary ethos of collaboration" that already exists between Scottish institutions (British Council Scotland 2013, 38). This is in contrast with the competition that is encouraged between providers in a marketised system.

The Scottish position on student information and performance measurement

The underlying value system in Scotland gives insight into why the post-2017 regulatory element of student information and performance measurement in England may not align well with the Scottish HE sector. In 2012–13, OAs were introduced as the principal mechanism by which institutions demonstrate their various commitments towards Scottish Government priorities, such as high-quality learning and teaching, and widening access. Each OA reflects the return that SFC and the Scottish Government expect for the public investment in FE and HE. The introduction of OAs was viewed sceptically in the Scottish sector and perceived as impinging upon institutional autonomy. However, the flexible approach to governance through OAs, including the role of the Outcome Agreement Manager (OAM), saw those fears subside initially (Riddell, Weddon, and Minty 2016, 24).

As the OA process evolved, however, SFC placed increasing importance on data and quantitative targets in the process to intensify the performance measurement aspect. The OA process was "intensified" by SFC on request of ministers from the 2017–18 cycle and this led to a focus on the National Performance Measures (NPMs) by which the university sector is judged, which caused some of these earlier concerns around the infringement of institutional autonomy to resurface. However, despite the increasing importance of data, OAs are largely qualitative documents and performance against NPMs is heavily contextualised by the knowledge and working relationships of the SFC OAMs. Institutions are required to set aspirational targets, or projections, against a number of key NPMs; these are collated by SFC to identify the sector position. The overall contribution of the sector in delivering improvements in areas such as widening access, gender equality, and graduate destinations is as important as the individual institution's performance.

Student information is also an area where there is increasing attention from the Scottish Government and the personalisation of student choice was a theme of the 15–24 Learner Journey Review. Recommendation 17 of the Learner Journey Review was to "develop better data and improve how existing data is used to support learners make the right choices for them", which is similar to intentions elsewhere in the UK (Scottish Government 2018). However, this is separate from performance measurement; the Scottish approach to using this data remains notably different from England's. Each year, SFC publishes a "Progress and Ambitions" report that presents the quantitative data submitted to SFC through the OAs, and which shows sector trends and projections towards the NPMs. The data from individual institutions is compared to identify where each could aspirationally contribute more, rather than compared and ranked with student consumers as the intended audience. The OA data is used to inform the consumer of progress and the return on their investment but in Scotland the consumer is primarily the Scottish Government, meaning that the priorities differ from those of individual students. Individual students have separate data and information sources on which to base their choice.

Despite the less market-oriented approach in Scotland, there are still compelling reasons why Scottish institutions should want to engage in and be included in the UK-wide HE sector. There are also compelling reasons why other UK institutions would want Scottish institutions to remain in the UK sector. These include attracting students, staff, and research funding – amongst others – due to the strength of the UK HE brand, to which Scottish institutions contribute significantly. Research has found that, while the Scottish education brand has a high profile, the UK education brand has a more prominent presence in some, although not all, international markets (British Council Scotland 2013). The Scottish sector benefits from its involvement in the UK HE brand, and this brand benefits from the inclusion of Scottish institutions.

The whole UK sector is of course also much larger than the Scottish sector, meaning UK-wide performance measures allow Scotland's nineteen HE institutions (HEIs) to evaluate their performance against the 128 English, 12 Welsh and 5 Northern Irish HEIs. This enables Scottish universities to measure and compare their performance to others which are similar in numerous differing ways which would not be available if limited to the Scottish sector, and the same applies for UK institutions comparing themselves to various Scottish institutions with which they compete for international students, for example. Additionally, OfS and the UK-wide data organisations have more resources to develop and innovate in this space than the Scottish sector would alone. This is naturally reflective of the size of the sectors but means that joined-up reporting can lead to more data expertise in the Scottish sector.

These reasons, along with the close history of the UK's HE sectors and the cross-border similarities and close relationship of some institutions, for example across the Russell Group institutions, are motivating factors for remaining in a UK-wide performance measurement and student information space. In 2006–07, a review of the UKPIs was conducted to ensure that the indicators remained fit for purpose in the changing HE context (NatCen and IES 2013, 2). The review restated the importance of the UK-wide coverage of the performance indicators, but a lot has changed since 2006–07.

The UK position on student information and performance measurement

Changes to the UK HE data landscape make student information an emerging area of divergence between the separate HE sectors, despite the shared history in this space. Debate began in the 1980s concerning the need for indicators to measure the performance of HEIs and a number of measures based on the data collected in the Universities Statistical Record (USR) were suggested (NatCen and IES 2013, 1). The first Performance Indicators (PIs) for the sectors were published in 1999 on behalf of the funding councils across the UK and they still exist today in an evolved form. Although the research focus of these exercises makes them fall outside the scope of this chapter, even earlier than this, the results of the first Research Selectivity Exercise (RSE), which became the Research Assessment Exercise (RAE) and then the Research Excellence Framework (REF) in 2014, were published in 1986.

Table 10.2 shows a timeline of key moments in the performance measurement and student information landscape, highlighting the pace of change in the most recent years. This pace of change, and the implication for the UK sector, is the focus of the following sections.

These notable moments in the timeline align with broader policy changes in the sector – the creation of USR in 1968 resulting from the Robbins report in 1963, the creation of HESA in 1993 with the 1992 Act, and now the recent changes with the 2017 Act (Youell 2017). However, these previous Acts have been UK-wide and linked to UK-wide policy whereas the Higher Education and Research Act 2017 has been introduced into a different policy context and is specific to England (though its remit on research has greater implications UK-wide). This means that the most recent additions, and the accelerated pace of change, to the UK student information timeline have largely arisen from changes to the HE policy agenda in England, including the creation of OfS and the definition of its purpose and role as distinct from its predecessor

Table 10.2 Scotland and England "student information" timeline

1968	Establishment of the Universities Statistical Record
Late 1980s	First league table published
1993	Creation of HESA
1994–95	First publication of HESA First Destinations Supplement
1999	First publication of institutional Performance Indicators (PIs), including statistical benchmarks, across the UK
2002–03	First UK Destination of Leavers from Higher Education (DLHE) survey, replacing the Destinations Supplement
2005	First National Student Survey (NSS)
2007–08	Review of UKPIs
2012	First Unistats
2017	First Teaching Excellence and Student Outcomes Framework ("TEF2") results
2018	Publication of Longitudinal Education Outcomes (LEO) on Unistats
	DLHE discontinued and replaced by Graduate Outcomes
	Publication of OfS Data Strategy
	Development of Taught Postgraduate Student Survey
	Review of Unistats
2019	Review of UKPIs
From 2019	Data Futures
	Subject-level TEF

funding council. This was then problematic for these performance metrics which operate in the existing shared performance measurement and student information space. Student information arrangements were overseen by a UK Student Information Advisory Group (SIAG), but this group went into abeyance in 2018 while new agreements and arrangements could be established reflecting the recent changes.

These changes and additions are often presented as a way of providing better information for students to make informed choices concerning the course and institution they should study at, to ensure they get value for money from their tuition fee spend. However, they are also a part of the data-driven approach to regulating the system where performance measurement is intrinsically linked to the increasing marketisation of the English HE policy agenda and to the view that the value of education can be judged in purely monetary terms. This is contrary to the value system still evident in the regulation of the Scottish sector, meaning involvement for Scotland in the same data measures is problematic. The 2016 White Paper *Success as a Knowledge Economy*, which set out the plans to establish OfS as the new "market regulator" stated that:

> By introducing more competition and informed choice into higher education, we will deliver better outcomes and value for students, employers and the taxpayers who underwrite the system. Competition between

providers in any market incentivises them to raise their game, offering consumers a greater choice of more innovative and better quality products and services at lower cost. Higher education is no exception.

(BIS 2016, 8)

This highlights how the two ideas, of better student information and market competition between institutions, are closely linked. One of the new duties of OfS is to encourage competition between providers for the benefits of student choice and the Competition and Markets Authority (CMA) takes an interest in how universities represent themselves: data in this sector is now "market sensitive". It may be assumed that the Scottish sector can do both: retain a less-marketised ethos and agenda for HE while participating in a UK-wide performance measurement and student information space. However, the power of data metrics to have unintended consequences, and to influence policy decisions, means that this is a complicated, and perhaps unachievable, goal. Inequality is an example of where these consequences will be felt as the market's effect is to exacerbate existing inequalities between different groups (Brown and Carasso 2013, 143). Despite the absence of a cap on student numbers, prospective students with more market power, in the form of wealth and connections, are better positioned to go to higher-status universities, resulting in an increase to their employability and market power. The market is driven, in large part, by the data informing the market, towards the needs of the majority and away from the minority. This is at odds with the Scottish Government's main priority for HE which is to achieve equity (Commission on Widening Access 2016).

Policy played out through data

The expansion of the use of data is unsurprising given the advances in analysis tools and the ability to capture huge amounts of data with relative ease. The use of these has expanded in the most recent years as shown in the timeline, but also in the expanding data infrastructure of QAA and Jisc, including sentiment analysis, predictive modelling, comparative data visualisation, and student benchmarking, "in ways that do appear to reinforce the ongoing marketisation of the sector" (Williamson 2018). There are clear examples of how the power of data metrics can have consequences on behaviour (O'Neil 2016) and the metrics underlying performance measurement and student information are no different. The outputs from these metrics become trusted as the truth on the subject being measured. The fact that Teaching Excellence and Student Outcomes Framework (TEF) scores, or average graduate salaries, are *proxies* for teaching and institution quality is overlooked; scores come to mean that the recipient institution is "poor quality", without having to take into account the full context. HE data metrics are also widely used by the media, as a more impactful way to tell the story than the underlying context. "Metric Power" is the idea that power is operationalised through algorithms and that algorithms then produce outcomes that become wider notions of truth (Beer 2017, 8). This is illustrated in the English sector with the rise in perception that student satisfaction and employment outcomes data accurately reflects excellence in HE (Williamson 2018). The focus on graduate outcomes then turns the ambitions of universities to the quantifiable destinations and salaries of their graduates and away from other key tenets such as the benefit of education as an end in itself, the production of knowledge, or high-quality institutions. Current metrics do not capture the personal growth of students and the graduate attributes, including communication, motivation, self-discipline, and critical thinking, which university education can instil. That which can be measured begins to take precedent.

One of the most pertinent questions of Metric Power is whether we are just measuring or if we are also shaping the thing being measured (Beer 2016). It has been argued that these metrics are increasingly prompting changes in organisational and individual behaviours in HE that will have a transformational impact on the sector, enabling it to see and act upon itself as a market (Williamson 2018). The metrics begin to cause changes in behaviour towards the outcomes that they measure and set, and since Scottish HE policy is increasingly not in pursuit of the same outcomes as the English HE sector then these potential influencers on behaviour should not be automatically welcomed by the Scottish HE sector. Understanding the underlying policy objectives is important for the Scottish sector in considering its engagement in performance measurement and student information metrics that originate in England. SFC is required by the Further and Higher Education (Scotland) Act 2005 to have regard to the UK and international context in which universities carry out their activities, but the pace and subtly complex nature of changes in this area mean that the necessary actions are not always clear.

How much separation is necessary?

This chapter has highlighted the differences in the underlying value systems of HE in the devolved nations of the UK and suggested that there is now a need to define the role of the UK-wide performance measurement and student information space in order to protect Scotland's distinct value system. The Scottish sector takes a cautious approach to engaging in the new data metrics and examples of this are outlined as follows:

- **TEF:** participation in TEF has been voluntary for Scottish universities and there were never any tuition fee conditions attached to participation in

Scotland. Five Scottish universities took part in TEF2. Scotland's universities have the QEF to ensure quality in learning and teaching.

- **NSS:** the survey has been used within the enhancement-led quality system in Scotland but its increased use as a regulatory tool in England poses challenges to its use in Scotland. OfS has considered changes and additions to the NSS, including running the survey at points other than the student's final year and, at the time of writing, is piloting a student survey for taught postgraduates in England. These changes are discussed UK-wide, but the outcomes may be English-specific, which would create presentational issues similar to non-participation in TEF.

- **Longitudinal Education Outcomes (LEO):** the LEO dataset is incredibly rich and provides an opportunity for extremely valuable analysis of the salaries of graduates. However, the LEO data's presentation as a means of judging an institution's quality is not something that aligns well with the Scottish sector. The LEO data was published on Unistats for English institutions in 2018 but Scotland opted out of this data being presented there for Scottish institutions. There is agreement in Scotland that the LEO data should be analysed in context, and should not form a basis for evaluating universities on its own.

It is possible that TEF could have a significant impact on Scottish universities if it becomes an influential marker of perceived teaching quality, potentially affecting the recruitment of students from the rUK and international students. Prospective students will likely not understand why there is different information available for institutions in different parts of the UK and it will be difficult to explain to prospective students why there are gaps in the information available for Scottish universities. In 2016–17, 13.1 per cent of undergraduate students at Scottish HEIs were from the rest of the UK, with 10.5 per cent of those from England (SFC 2018a, Table 21) and the sector is aware of the importance of not limiting the ability to recruit these students.

These developments have resulted in the establishment of a student information group in Scotland that brings together sector representatives with expertise in planning and quality together with stakeholders. This has helped to build consensus within the Scottish context on responding to developments from England and OfS. However, responding to each change as it arises is not an ideal policy position and there may be merit in Scotland developing an overarching policy on performance measurement and student information that responds appropriately to the changing policy intentions in England. Scotland primarily needs arrangements that support the requirements of the Scottish Government and the sector for robust performance information, and these are becoming quite different from what is required in rUK.

David Beer highlights that "it's not necessarily the measure itself that has power, but how it is realised and integrated into practices, decisions and processes" (2016, 78). This may mean that Scotland can still share a UK-wide performance measurement and student information space, but only if Scottish policy can appropriately dictate how these metrics are realised and integrated into practice, decisions, and processes in Scotland. SFC reviews its own arrangements for quality assessment in a separate, but parallel, process to the rest of the UK (Hefce 2015), suggesting that Scotland could also develop a separate but parallel approach to student information. Ideally this would allow a shared UK space to continue but does not commit the Scottish sector to participating in metrics that are driving an agenda that is not aligned with its own.

This chapter highlights lessons for policymakers across the UK for operating in the shared UK policy spaces. First, data and quantitative student information are becoming increasingly important and the power of these measures to influence policy must be understood. Second, policymakers in each country need to think carefully about the UK context that they operate in. For England, this is to consider the spill-over effect of its policy decisions due to its domination of the UK sector, and for Scotland and the other devolved administrations, it is to understand not only their own context but what's going on in England. Given the proximity and shared history of the sectors, remaining close and aligned is crucial, but for Scotland it can't be at the cost of losing its core values.

References

Beer, D (2016) *Metric Power.* London: Macmillan.
Beer, D (2017) The social power of algorithms. *Information, Communication and Society*, 20(1), 1–13.
BIS (2016) *Success as a Knowledge Economy: Teaching Excellence, Social Mobility and Student Choice.* London: Department for Business, Innovation and Skills
British Council Scotland (2013) *A Strategic Analysis of the Scottish Higher Education Sector's Distinctive Assets.* Edinburgh: British Council Scotland. Available from: scotland.britishcouncil.org/sites/default/files/scotland-report-a-strategic-analysis-of-the-scottish-higher-education-sectors-distinctive-assets.pdf
Brown, R. and H Carasso (2013) *Everything for Sale? The Marketisation of UK Higher Education.* London: Routledge.
Bruce, T (2012) *Universities and Constitutional Change in the UK: The Impact of Devolution on the Higher Education Sector.* Oxford: Higher Education Policy Institute. Available from: www.hepi.ac.uk/2012/04/16/universities-and-constitutional-change-in-the-uk-the-impact-of-devolution-on-the-higher-education-sector/

Commission on Widening Access (2016) *A Blueprint for Fairness.* Edinburgh: Scottish Government Offices. Available from: www.gov.scot/publications/ blueprint-fairness-final-report-commission-widening-access/

Hefce (2015) *Future Approaches to Quality Assessment in England, Wales and Northern Ireland.* Bristol: Higher Education Funding Council for England. Available from: dera.ioe.ac.uk/23416/1/2015_11_.pdf

NatCen and IES (2013) *How Should We Measure Higher Education? A Fundamental Review of Performance Indicators. Part Two: The Evidence Report.* Brighton: Institute for Employment Studies. Available from: dera.ioe. ac.uk/18967/2/2013_ukpireview2.pdf

O'Neil, C (2016) *Weapons of Math Destruction: How Big Data Increases Inequality and Threatens Democracy.* New York: Crown.

Raffe, D and L Croxford (2013) How stable is the stratification of higher education in England and Scotland? *British Journal of Sociology of Education,* 36(2), 313–335.

Riddell, S, E Weddon, and S Minty (2016) *Higher Education in Scotland and the UK: Diverging or Converging Systems.* Edinburgh: Edinburgh University Press.

Scottish Government Offices (2018) *15–24 Learner Journey Review.* Edinburgh: Scottish Government Offices. Available from: www.gov.scot/ publications/15-24-learner-journey-review-9781788518741/

SFC (2015) *Scottish Funding Council Strategic Plan* 2015–18. Edinburgh: Scottish Funding Council. Available from: www.sfc.ac.uk/publications-statistics/ corporate-publications/corporate-publications-2015/SFCCP022015.aspx

SFC (2017) *Scottish Funding Council Guidance to Higher Education Institutions on Quality from August 2017–2022.* Edinburgh: Scottish Funding Council. Available from: www.sfc.ac.uk/web/FILES/guidance_sfcgd112017/SFCGD 112017-SFC-guidance-HE-institutions-quality.pdf

SFC (2018a) *Higher Education Students and Qualifiers 2016–17.* Edinburgh: Scottish Funding Council. Available from: www.sfc.ac.uk/publications-statistics/statistical-publications/statistical-publications-2018/SFCST042018. aspx

SFC (2018b) *University Outcome Agreement Guidance 2019–20.* Edinburgh: Scottish Funding Council. Available from: www.sfc.ac.uk/web/FILES/ guidance_sfcgd212018/SFCGD212018_University_Outcome_Agreement_ Guidance_2019-20.pdf

Williams, G (2004) The higher education market in the United Kingdom. In: P Teixeira, B Jongbloed, D Dill, and A Amaral, eds. *Markets in Higher Education, Higher Education Dynamics,* Volume 6. Dordrecht: Springer.

Williamson, B (2018, 26 September) *The Mutating Metric Machinery of Higher Education.* Available from: codeactsineducation.wordpress.com/2018/09/26/ metric-machinery-of-higher-education/

Youell, A (2017) A brief history of higher education data. *Wonkhe.* Available from: wonkhe.com/blogs/a-brief-history-of-higher-education-data/.

PART 3

Institutions' engagement with policy

CHAPTER 11

A study in imperfection
Five lessons on how to influence with impact
Colette Fletcher

Introduction

For me, the importance of informing and influencing policy has always been grounded in the role of universities to support the public good. It is a thought that I have clung to closely as the narrative around the higher education (HE) sector has shifted more and more towards preparing students for the world of work and the financial value that a degree brings to the individual. I firmly believe that we have a duty to remind policymakers and those in government that HE is not only a transformational, life-changing experience for the students, but that the consequences of HE have far-reaching implications and benefits for society more widely. One could argue that the stakes have never been higher. Since 2012, we have seen a proliferation of new HE initiatives on a scale hitherto unheard of in England, including the introduction of the Teaching Excellence and Student Outcomes Framework (TEF), the Knowledge Exchange Framework (KEF), and the Longitudinal Education Outcomes (LEO) data, to name but a few.

Attempting to influence and inform public policy amid this cornucopia of initiatives can be simultaneously rewarding and frustrating. Once primarily the domain of civil servants and those working within the HE sector organisations, representative bodies, and mission groups, there are few universities nowadays that are not actively engaged in the HE policy agenda, often driven by vice-chancellors and supported by large and experienced teams behind the scenes. In such a crowded and jostling policy environment it is more important than ever to influence with impact and make sure your message is heard. At a time when resources and funding in HE are coming under increasing pressure, it is also important for all those who are influencing and informing policy to demonstrate the value of their work by clearly and concisely communicating the outcomes.

This chapter puts forward five key points of learning to try and help those who are informing and influencing policy to make an impact. Each lesson is exemplified by a quote from a well-known public figure and draws on both research and personal experience. The lessons explore everything from the importance of institutional culture in informing and influencing policy, to how best to communicate about policy outcomes.

Lesson One – In an imperfect world, have the confidence to be yourself

> Public policy is a study in imperfection. It involves imperfect people, with imperfect information, making deeply imperfect choices.
>
> Jake Sullivan – former Deputy Assistant to President Obama and National Security Advisor to Vice President Joe Biden

This is possibly the most important lesson for anyone working in HE policy: the system is not perfect and that can lead to unpredictability. Even if you do everything right – for example, you have a clear evidence-based approach, your communications have been appropriately tailored for your audience, and you are working with the right people at the right time – it is still entirely possible that you will fail to have impact due to circumstances completely outside your control, such as a political trade-off or compromise behind the scenes. You have to learn to roll with the punches, because you won't win them all.

Beyond the normal failings of human beings, which can include innate biases, resistance to change, and the favouring of pre-existing prejudices (all of which are major factors to think about when trying to influence and inform policy), it can be especially challenging working with policymakers because they have myriad calls on their time, and they also live in a transient world. At the time of writing there has been a series of high-profile Cabinet and ministerial resignations linked to Brexit negotiations, including Universities and Science Minister Sam Gyimah. While coverage has understandably focused on the reasons behind the departures, the impact it will have on general policymaking should not be underestimated. There is also an important learning point here: it can be tempting to focus on the key movers and shakers of the time, but politics is a fickle world and stars shine and wane with alarming frequency. Never neglect the opposition, and try and build a contacts list that includes up-and-coming policymakers as well as the old hands, otherwise your career will only last as long as theirs does.

To give yourself the best chance of influencing with impact, you really need to understand your audience. What are their priorities? What constraints are they working within? Are they going to be the person making the decision or the person advising the person who will be making the decision? This last point is important because in my experience, the former wants a one-page briefing of key points, whilst the latter will expect to see the research and evidence that backs up your points as well. It is important to work out what your audience wants, and make sure you give them what they need. Don't ever send your advocates into battle unarmed.

Once you have identified your audience, your next task is to get in front of them. Given that there is no "right" way, the key thing is to be creative and flexible. Use all of the contacts at your disposal, whether they are political links fostered by your leadership team, high-ranking governors and board members, high-profile alumni, or the combined forces of the sector mission groups and representative bodies. The key is not to be afraid to be creative in order to catch someone's attention – in the wide sea of voices clamouring to be heard it is important to stand out if you want to inform and influence. The take-home message from this lesson is that in this imperfect world, you need to have the confidence to be yourself – informing and influencing is about building trust, and to do that you must be authentic and credible.

Lesson Two – Make sure you understand the bigger picture

> The one who adapts his policy to the times prospers, and likewise … the one whose policy clashes with the demands of the times does not.
>
> Niccolo Machiavelli, *The Prince*

To ensure that your work informing and influencing policy has impact, it is important to recognise and understand the political context and wider HE policy environment that you are working in. Ever since the late 1970s UK HE has been undergoing something of a policy revolution. This stemmed from the "massification" that followed the Robbins Report in 1963 as the sector adapted and evolved to meet the needs of a growing population in which a much higher proportion went on to study in universities. In the mid-1980s there were fewer than 60 universities in the UK sector and the average rate of participation amongst 18-year-olds was 6 per cent (Foskett 2011). In 2017 there were 162 HE institutions in receipt of public funding serving 48 per cent of England's population of 18-year-olds (UUK 2017) alongside a decreasing number of mature students. This growth has been accompanied by an increase in overseas students. In the mid-1980s approximately 20,000 international students studied in the UK; in 2015–16 this had increased to more than 310,000 (ibid.). This expansion was driven by the importance of HE for the UK's economic success and its role in improving social mobility, at a time when the world was facing severe economic challenges as a result of falling oil prices and the decline of traditional industries and manufacturing in the West (Foskett 2011). In 1976 the Prime Minister, James Callaghan, gave a speech at Ruskin College that started a national debate about the purpose of HE in the UK (Callaghan 1976). The rhetoric of the day linked the global economic crisis to a lack of skills and knowledge that could only be addressed through government intervention to grow the educational system and produce more highly skilled graduates.

The proposed mechanism for achieving this growth without significant additional public expenditure, and without sacrificing quality, was marketisation. Milton Friedman (1962) and Friedrich von Hayek (1976) describe how consumer choice can drive competition between institutions, and how the constant need to gain an advantage can lead to innovation, efficiencies, and an increase in standards. Marketisation has since been actively encouraged and fuelled by a number of government policies from the main political parties (for examples, see *Higher Ambitions: The Future of Universities in a Knowledge Economy* (BIS 2009); the Browne Review (Browne 2010), and *Success as a Knowledge Economy: Teaching Excellence, Social Mobility and Student Choice* (BIS 2016)) and is still the main principle underpinning current HE policy development today.

This can be a real challenge for those trying to inform and influence HE policy, as many of us are deeply concerned about the effects of increasing marketisation. The key learning point is that you need to find a balance between recognising the importance of marketisation as an influencer, while also mitigating some of its least desirable effects.

Lesson Three – Don't underestimate the importance of institutional culture

> I am not afraid of an army of lions led by a sheep; I am afraid of an army of sheep led by a lion.
>
>   Attributed to Alexander the Great

Institutional culture is incredibly important when trying to inform and influence policy. First, it affects how policy work is approached within an institution. Many vice-chancellors are actively engaged in politics and in informing and influencing policy, and there is little doubt that when this is a priority it permeates throughout the institution. The introduction of impact case studies in the Research Excellence Framework (REF) has also brought greater appreciation of the value of this kind of work, and there are now numerous teams and research centres around the country dedicated to researching the policymaking process, including several specialising in HE policy. Often the desire to inform and influence HE policy stems from institutional strategy – what is important to the institution and how is this reflected in the current political discourse? When there is discord between institutional priorities and the political narrative, it is time for policy teams to swing into action. It is also important to note that this tieback to institutional strategy is very important when it comes to demonstrating the value of informing and influencing policy – this kind of work can sometimes be intangible and it is not enough to simply bring about change; you need to demonstrate how this change links to the institution's strategy and objectives.

There is another challenge that you will face when trying to inform and influence policy – how do you balance the need to be transparent and to demonstrate impact with the need to be discreet and to retain the trust of those whose problems you are attempting to solve? You may want to shout about your recent successes but, as noted earlier, effective informing and influencing is about building trust. Sometimes it is better to quietly reflect on a job well done rather than to seek recognition or reward.

Institutional culture can also make things more complicated at a national level. One of my biggest concerns about the marketisation of the HE sector was that it could lead to a reduction in collaboration between institutions. This was already a tricky enough proposition, but the HE sector has become increasingly diverse and there is often no clear single point of view on current issues. In these circumstances, coming to an agreed position for lobbying purposes is becoming nigh on impossible, and I would argue that the sector is the weaker for it. We have effectively hamstrung our mission groups through our inability to find common ground, and I suspect it is no coincidence that they then struggle to define their role in the ever-changing HE environment. The same is true of our representative bodies, which must be cautious about which issues to engage with for fear of not acting in the best interests of their members.

When confronted with the consequences of the increased regulation and marketisation of English HE following the Higher Education and Research Act of 2017, it is not uncommon for people to ask, "but why didn't the universities do something about it? Why did you let it get this far?" My honest answer is that I think institutional culture may have got the better of us. Increasing competition caused by marketisation has encouraged many of us to become too insular and to spend too much time on introspection, and our institutional culture has become about survival. I am fortunate enough to work for a university that encourages us to think beyond our own walls and about what is in the best interests of the sector and society, but I suspect that this is a luxury that comes from a position of strength and financial stability.

Rather than a learning point as such, the take-home message from this lesson is really more of a warning: as a passionate and dedicated member of staff who wants to inform and influence policy, you are not just a product of your institutional culture. You shape it. You define it. To paraphrase Alexander the Great – be a lion, not a sheep.

Lesson Four – Present solutions, not problems

> My policy on cake is pro having it and pro eating it.
>
> Boris Johnson – Member of Parliament for Uxbridge
> and South Ruislip, former Mayor of London and former
> Secretary of State for Foreign and Commonwealth Affairs

This is a horrible cliché, but there is a lot of truth behind it. The decision-makers that you are trying to influence are busy people and it is simply not helpful or constructive to flag up all the issues you have with a particular policy without putting forward some ideas for how to fix them. In addition, you have spent a considerable amount of time researching these issues and thinking about them (or the people you are working with have) and therefore your ideas and suggestions will likely be perceived as having a particular value, as long as you have presented yourself as a trusted and credible source.

Good communication is key when presenting your solutions. It is therefore important to be tenacious, and to constantly and consistently reinforce your messages. As previously discussed, you need to consider your audience, but generally speaking, proposals should be concise and easily understandable with few or no acronyms, jargon, or technical language. Key messages should be clearly defined, and soundbites can be useful as catchy hooks to draw people in. Authenticity in communication is very important – not just authentic to you as an individual, but also to your institution's culture and values.

It may sound obvious, but the key to good communication when informing and influencing policy is understanding how the various policymaking processes work. Many people working in policy gain this through a degree in politics, but for anyone who comes to policymaking via another route your best starting point is the UK Treasury's Green Book. This sets out the policymaking cycle and how the process is appraised and evaluated by government. However, it portrays an overly simplistic model: the reality is much more fluid and dynamic. To help you get to grips with that fluidity and dynamism, I would recommend the material and training courses available from the Institute for Government. Their projects and reports cover everything from choice and competition in public service markets to "making policy better". These resources really help you get inside the mind of government and policymakers and understand how things work and what is important to them.

There are also lots of tools and frameworks out there to help you communicate and influence with impact. In my opinion the best resources are available from the National Co-ordinating Centre for Public Engagement (NCCPE). Their website includes an excellent "getting started" guide, lots of top tips and hints, and links to lots of useful information about your likely policy audiences and how you should go about engaging with them. For help and advice on influencing HE policy specifically, the Society for Research into Higher Education (SRHE) has a Higher Education Policy Network that provides a forum for the discussion of HE research and policy issues, as well as numerous training and continuous professional development events, and access to research publications.

The learning point here is to take the time to understand the policy environment so that you know the best time to make your intervention. Once you have taken the plunge, communicate your solutions confidently and with authenticity.

Lesson Five – Engineer your impact

> It's amazing what doors can open if you reach out to people with a smile, friendly attitude, and a desire to make a positive impact.
>
> Richard Branson – entrepreneur, and founder of the Virgin brand

The effects of policies can be indirect and are often not immediately obvious. It is also entirely possible that a policy will not produce any effects that are directly measurable or attributable. It doesn't help that historically quite a lot of policymaking has been based on a standard model of economics, which is now largely recognised as redundant in human decision-making. Human beings are rarely particularly logical or rational, which is important to bear in mind when you are trying to inform and influence policy. The use of behavioural economics in policymaking has become more prevalent since the establishment of the Behavioural Insights Team (sometimes known as the "nudge unit") in 2010. *MINDSPACE: Influencing Behaviour Through Public Policy* was published by the Institute for Government and the Cabinet Office in 2010 (Dolan, Hallsworth, Halpern, King, and Vlaev 2010), and explores how behaviour change theory can help meet current policy challenges. The Behavioural Insights Team was established shortly afterwards to generate and apply behavioural insights to inform policy, improve public services, and deliver results for citizens and society. *Behavioural Government – Using Behavioural Science to Improve How Governments Make Decisions* builds on the Behavioural Insights Team's work and was published in 2018 (Hallsworth, Egan, Rutter, and McCrae 2018). It explores how policymakers are influenced by the same heuristics and biases that they try to address by using behavioural science in policymaking, and how these biases can be addressed and/or mitigated. Both of these reports are essential reading for anyone working to inform and influence policy. Behavioural economics and behavioural science can be very useful tools for demonstrating impact. They can lead to better outcomes, for less money, than more conventional policy tools. Using behavioural economics to engineer specific outcomes can also help create tangible and measurable outcomes for your policy work.

The take-home message from this lesson is that it can be very hard to demonstrate impact, but you can engineer it. The way in which you plan and design your informing and influencing work, and the methods that you use, can all affect the impact that you have.

Conclusion

Informing and influencing policy is an imperfect science. It can be intensely rewarding and exceedingly frustrating at the same time, but I hope these five lessons, based on research and my own experience, will push you closer to the former rather than the latter.

1. **Have the confidence to be yourself** – informing and influencing is about building trust, and to do that you must be authentic and credible.
2. **Make sure you understand the bigger picture** – you need to find a balance between recognising the importance of marketisation as an influencer, while also mitigating some of its least desirable effects.
3. **Don't underestimate the importance of institutional culture** – be a lion, not a sheep.
4. **Present solutions, not problems** – know the best time to make your intervention and communicate your solutions confidently and with authenticity.
5. **Engineer your impact** – the way in which you plan and design your informing and influencing work, and the methods that you use, can all affect the impact that you have.

References

BIS (2009) *Higher Ambitions: The Future of Universities in a Knowledge Economy.* London: Department for Business, Innovation and Skills.

BIS (2016) *Success as a Knowledge Economy: Teaching Excellence, Social Mobility and Student Choice.* London: Department for Business, Innovation and Skills.

Browne, J (2010) *Securing a Sustainable Future for Higher Education: An Independent Review of Higher Education Funding & Student Finance.* London: Department for Business, Innovation and Skills.

Callaghan, J (1976) The Ruskin College speech, 18 October 1976. In: J Ahler, B Cosin and M Hales, eds. *Diversity and Change: Education Policy and Selection.* London: Routledge.

Dolan, P, M Hallsworth, D Halpern, D King, and I Vlaev (2010) *MINDSPACE: Influencing Behaviour Through Public Policy.* London: Cabinet Office and Institute for Government.

Foskett, N (2011) Markets, government, funding and the marketisation of UK higher education. In: M Molesworth, R Scullion, and E Nixon, eds. *The Marketisation of Higher Education and the Student as Consumer.* London: Routledge.

Friedman, M (1962) *Capitalism and Freedom.* Chicago, IL: Chicago University Press.

Hallsworth, M, M Egan, J Rutter, and J McCrae (2018) *Behavioural Government: Using Behavioural Science to Improve How Governments Make Decisions.* London: Behavioural Insights Ltd.

Hayek, F von (1976) *Law, Legislation and Liberty: Vol. 2 Rules and Order.* London: Routledge and Kegan Paul.

Robbins, LC (1963) *Higher Education: Report of the Committee.* London: HMSO.

UUK (2017) *Higher Education in Facts and Figures 2017.* London: Universities UK.

CHAPTER 12

Punching above your weight

Establishing a policy and public affairs function in a modern university

Jessica Strenk

Introduction

At a higher education (HE) sector conference on public affairs, I found myself on my feet as the chair asked the audience to stand up if they worked in a newly created public affairs role. This exercise effectively showed how quickly public affairs had grown as a profession in the HE sector over the preceding two to three years. We are a new breed of communications professionals in UK universities. In a diverse sector, much of the recent growth represented by the dozens of delegates on their feet is to be found in younger universities where a public affairs function is often being set up for the first time. These roles may involve other responsibilities such as policy, media relations, community engagement, corporate communications, and supporting a vice-chancellor. They may also be part-time roles.

Many younger universities are faced with the challenge of staying financially afloat in an increasingly competitive market for students and a difficult external environment. It is likely that there will be limited resources available, be it budgets for events, consultancy support, training, publications, or research reports. As such, sessions led by representatives from older institutions with established public affairs functions and teams, with the role well understood and with a track-record of successful impact, felt quite distant from my own experiences and role. Impressive presentations on ministerial visits to research facilities and hospitals, glossy publications and glamorous events in Parliament with high-profile alumni abounded. There is a limit to how much this part of the new HE public affairs community could learn from public affairs colleagues in more established and better-funded settings and it is in this spirit that I offer up my reflections and experience of setting up a new policy and public affairs function in a modern university. I aim to support the large community of policy and public affairs professionals who are starting from scratch in cash-strapped parts of the sector, the one-man or one-woman bands who are establishing the role for the first time in their university and who need to demonstrate value with limited resource and support.

It is now essential that this part of the sector builds its capacity and is effective in its policy and public affairs work. Since I began my role in spring 2017 the English HE sector has experienced massive turbulence and change, from the Brexit vote to the introduction of a new regulatory framework, an unexpected General Election to the announcement of a review of post-18 education and funding. The sector has also faced unprecedented criticism and disdain as students, parents, and the media question the value of HE amid rising tuition fees and vice-chancellors' pay, concerns about graduate debt, the Government's reforms to technical education, and the apprenticeships agenda. Wales has seen the implementation of the Diamond reforms to funding, and in Scotland there is a continued squeeze on public funds to Scottish universities. More than ever, commentators are questioning the role of younger universities and what they have to offer. I still frequently hear people ask "What's the point of post-92s? Was it a mistake to grant these institutions university status in the first place?" at high-profile policy discussions on HE. Likewise, the tabloids regularly report inaccurately and sensationally on perceived "low-value" degrees, retention rates, or graduate salaries for students at younger universities. It is critical that public affairs colleagues in that part of the sector are working as efficiently and effectively as possible to demonstrate the value and contribution of this part of the sector for students, society, and the economy.

My role as Policy and Public Affairs manager for Middlesex University London is based in the communications team, line-managed by the Associate Director for External Relations and Stakeholder Engagement, and has a direct line of report to the Vice-Chancellor. The role was advertised as full-time, but I negotiated to work a four-day week to allow me time with my young family. With a new vice-chancellor at the helm, Middlesex was refining its five-year strategy and took building support for its mission as a key strategic aim. Partly in response to the volatile external environment and increasing pressure on university finances, the university was keen to play a more influential role in external policy debates and to secure decisions and resources to support its aims. Middlesex has a strong mission to widen participation and celebrate its diverse learning environment as a resource and graduate asset, where many of its students are the first in their families to enter HE. Engaged in the Government's industrial strategy agenda, the university is committed to boosting social mobility and productivity through innovative, practice-based provision, creating the skills employers need for the fourth industrial revolution. As well as the skills agenda, the university was keen to increase its influence on HE debates affecting the whole sector, such as Brexit and the new regulatory framework for HE. The role would involve engagement at local, regional, and national level, dipping into local politics at times on planning and community issues.

It was with trepidation that I arrived for my first day in spring 2017 and stood in the university's buzzy and bright central quad. What follows are my insights based on two years in the role of a new public affairs professional in the younger, less well-represented part of the sector. I do not claim to have all the answers, nor to have got everything right, but I have worked hard to establish a brand-new function and make an impact on policy in the areas the university cares about, enhancing its reputation among decision-makers. I simply hope that my experiences may be easier to relate to and more reflective of the situation of most of my peers across UK universities, providing ideas to reinterpret in their own settings, comfort, and reassurance at times, and cautionary tales of things to avoid.

Establish the trust of the senior team

A large proportion of my first year in the post has been spent establishing relationships, working my way around the institution, getting to know the personalities and who does what. Top of the to-do list has to be getting some time with each member of the leadership team. This is about understanding the perspectives, priorities, and personal styles of the senior colleagues you will be working closely with. Where is their expertise? How do they communicate? Can they help you pull together a policy position? Could they get over key messages to a minister or select committee? Colleagues will also be more interested to meet you if they believe you can add value to *their* role. For example, can you help them get traction on an issue they care about? Could you enhance their standing in the sector by developing a blog on a key policy issue together? Can you help them prepare for challenging external meetings or represent them when they are unable to attend? Getting to know these people and how you can collaborate will build your own profile among the institution's leadership team. It is also important to avoid assuming that people understand what public affairs is or how it fits with their own work. Remember the confused look you see in people's eyes when you meet people outside work and tell them what you do. When the function is new in a university, explaining your role to the university's leaders, what it is trying to achieve, and how it might support their own goals and interests is more important than ever.

Find your experts

Equally important is to invest time in the layer of directors and senior managers in a university's faculties and professional services. These are the experts who can provide the public affairs professional with the evidence and insight that help to influence and build credibility for the university in the eyes of decision-makers. Get these relationships right and this pool of colleagues can help you to do your job more efficiently, feeding you the information you need when you need it, and explaining the details of complex issues when you are short on time to get your head around them. They also provide the detail on what the university does well and less well so that you are able to showcase the best bits and defend weaknesses with robust arguments. For me it is Simon, Head of Planning, who analyses data and runs focus groups with commuter students on their specific needs and challenges which can provide the bedrock of thought leadership work, or Darryll, Director of Apprenticeships and Skills, who is established in the sector, and with government, as an expert in practice-based learning and apprenticeships. There is also Mark, the Head of Knowledge Transfer, who worked in the Cabinet Office and has an exhaustive understanding of the London skills-and-knowledge transfer landscape.

So many of these colleagues are already engaging in public affairs activity through their professional networks and membership of external organisations. They have often been doing a great job in quietly influencing policy-making by themselves before you came along. There may be value you can add, for example by putting them in touch with contacts, briefing them for external meetings, providing them with platforms, or linking them up with journalists with an interest in their agendas. At the same time, it is important to remain humble and avoid positioning yourself as the only source of public affairs wisdom through which all activity should pass. Such an approach could inadvertently reduce capacity and alienate and frustrate colleagues already doing valuable work. Make time to have coffee with these people, be curious about what they do and you will reap the benefits.

Identify key assets

Another important resource for public affairs colleagues in the younger part of the sector are the university's key assets, its unique selling points that will tempt decision-makers to engage with you. Keep your ear to the ground about what is going on in the university so you can get a feel for these. This could be an academic expert in a particularly important policy area or a senior leader, governor, or alumnus who communicates with charm and passion. It could be a ground-breaking project with high-profile partners on STEM outreach in disadvantaged communities. It could also be a physical entity in the form of a research facility, a new building, a living wall, or an industry-standard media or animation studio. Never underestimate the impact of your students and apprentices on decision-makers who, without fail, are enthused and inspired by hearing authentic, human stories about the impact your university has had on them or their perspective on government policy.

It is after all the younger part of the sector which is disproportionately supporting the most disadvantaged learners to access higher-level learning. The stories behind our students need to be heard; they are compelling when they are told. Mindful that Middlesex is just a stone's throw from Westminster and Whitehall, for those based beyond easy striking distance of the capital or Edinburgh, Cardiff, or Belfast, it is important to make it as easy as possible for decision-makers to engage with your university. There is a strong will to connect with universities beyond the South East so when it is not possible to tempt influencers to your campus, showing creativity in taking your university to London may be needed. This doesn't have to be a glamorous Parliament take-over but could be as simple as offering to organise a seminar for civil servants on a particular topic of interest.

Share your work

Another key lesson I have learned is the importance of sharing my work internally. When establishing a brand-new function in a university, it is more important than ever to share the work you are doing, communicate with colleagues at all levels and establish links and connections across areas of work as broadly as possible. Determined to make an impact while also working part-time with a young family, there have been busy times when I have come to the office, got my head down, gone to meetings and rushed out the door again. I have at times missed out on making links with other colleagues' work and unconsciously left them out of the loop on my own activities. Regular meetings and reminder alerts in my diary are helping me to do this more consistently, and I am already benefiting as other colleagues, from media to internal communications, outreach and education liaison to planning, support and inform my work as I am able to enhance theirs.

Sharing internally is also about alerting staff across the university about the work you are doing externally on behalf of the institution they work for. At Middlesex, a staff survey revealed that the external policy environment was felt to be a key risk and concern for many of our academic staff. Colleagues did not feel up to speed with external developments that might affect the university and were unaware of the work we were engaged in to influence them. This was a trigger to communicate more proactively through internal communications channels, such as staff newsletters and the intranet, about the public affairs activity the institution is engaged in to mitigate these risks. A short update in a weekly newsletter can go a long way in demonstrating the university's national or regional influencing activity and raising your own profile. I have avoided creating a regular update devoted to public affairs which is simply not feasible with limited resource, and in any case not always needed at quieter times in the political and academic cycle. When I do send email updates round, I know that staff engage with them, as they are timely and relevant and only come when there is something important to say. Sessions on public affairs at staff conferences and departmental meetings have been well attended and received. I have found it also worked well to bring in external speakers on HE public affairs, for example from Universities UK, Wonkhe, or a mission group, to speak to colleagues about developments. This can bring a fresh perspective and provoke interesting discussion on the university's role and position.

Perhaps the most important reason to share your work is to demonstrate impact. These days few sectors are immune to restructuring and cost-cutting exercises but working in a new area that may not be well understood one can feel particularly vulnerable. Public affairs is often viewed as a bit of a "dark art" and its impact can be difficult to measure, but in these cash-strapped times complacency is not an option. Having done the groundwork to build networks and relationships of trust across the institution will go a long way towards this. However, considering the role of metrics and key performance indicators, it is important to demonstrate what you have achieved for the institution and how you have had impact externally if your role is to survive and grow. Consultancies can offer to assess your impact for the cost of your annual salary. A baseline survey of key stakeholders, for example in Parliament, and their understanding of your university to measure progress against later, seems unlikely to be worth the investment; I have seen little evidence that it results in higher profile.

When time and resource are tight it is essential to be clear who the most important stakeholders are and focus efforts on them. This may only be a handful of key decision-makers for whom you can measure impact and increase engagement. I have found a more cost-effective approach is to plan carefully, map your stakeholders and influencers, set yourself targets, and then demonstrate how you have met your objectives. Quantitative measures of meetings with decision-makers, visits to campus, numbers of guests at events, consultation responses, sector policy consultations, and select committee submissions are part of this picture. Be bold about how you have influenced policy change or contributed to change working with other stakeholders. Squirrel away a folder of testimonials and positive feedback to add a more qualitative and human touch when demonstrating how your role is supporting the institution's strategic objectives.

Make the most of the university's partners

A public affairs role must also face outwards and engage externally, and university partnerships can provide a helpful route to getting noticed and punching above your weight. Teaming up with a partner – be it a high-profile employer, a local school, a further education (FE) college, or local rugby team – can add weight to a policy intervention, for example by presenting a unified perspective from two or more key actors. Middlesex's relationship with FE colleges has caught the eye of ministers and high-profile MPs. The university's partnership with Saracens, a premiership rugby club, including delivery of its sport science programmes at their stadium and opening a free school, plays into two key government agendas. There is scope to elevate these collaborations in public affairs activity through joint submissions, events, and campaigns where sharing resource and expertise can help both the institution and its partner to gain traction with decision-makers. I would also include your students' union in this list. Ours happens to be award-winning and expert in campaigning on local issues and conducting national level research in collaboration with the National Union of Students. Getting to know the chief executive and sabbatical officers helps you to stay up to speed on students' perspectives on policymaking. Meeting with decision-makers alongside a students' union representative is particularly powerful and something I am hoping to do more of.

Use your membership organisations

Most universities are members of one of the national and regional representative bodies or mission groups for UK universities. While the fragmentation of the sector between mission groups and non-aligned institutions often weakens its voice in policy debates, there are benefits to be reaped for the smaller institution working to have impact through its public affairs activity. Membership subscriptions to these organisations do not come cheap and many universities are sensibly reviewing these closely to consider whether they add enough value, so it is important to make them work for your role if you are a member. Get to know the public affairs teams and the policy leads in the areas that are important to your university. They can often save your skin and a lot of time and energy by providing a quick steer or update by email or over the phone on an issue. Highlight areas of work that matter to your institution and spearhead activity through these groupings so they add their resource to your public affairs goals.

Encouraging your senior team to engage in the policy network groups and activities can create platforms and opportunities to feed in case studies and evidence of the issues that matter to your institution that would otherwise be hard to access. Strong links with the media and communications team can get your university onto the list of institutions to ask for media comment, draft blogs, or provide case studies or filming locations. Depending on your institution's profile, if you are not already members consider making the case for membership of national and regional business organisations, such as the Confederation of British Industry (CBI) and chambers of commerce, who now count many universities among their members. These groups also have important expertise that can support your work and provide platforms with business and government that you may otherwise struggle to develop in a younger institution.

Target key decision-makers

Doing public affairs for a small fish in the big pond that is the UK HE sector, you cannot hope to reach all the decision-makers with a stake in HE and skills policy, so it is important to be clear about the most important objectives for your university and target your energy wisely. For example, Middlesex has grown its relationships with its local MPs since I arrived which has been invaluable in giving us access to ministers and committee chairs. We have also submitted to committee inquiries and given oral evidence – alongside one of our robots, no less – to the education select committee, which has been great for our national and global profile and provided a springboard for engagement. Equally important has been to seek to cultivate relationships with relevant ministers, special advisors, senior local/regional and government officials, and government agencies.

Consider models of working

If you have control over it, then it is worth reflecting carefully about where you sit within the university structure and your model of working. There is a fault line between those public affairs colleagues who sit alongside the vice-chancellor and/or executive team and those who are part of the wider communications operation. Having initially regretted that I did not have the status of sitting with the leadership team, I really value the proximity I have to media, corporate, and internal communications, alumni, content, and marketing teams. As well as the camaraderie and social advantages of sitting within a large professional services department, this arrangement helps me to work closely with these colleagues who are so important in supporting my work. There are other models in the sector which are worth a thought where, for example, the public affairs role is shared with the local economic partnership. This original arrangement has the potential to have a big impact in a region and subsequently opens more doors to decision-makers.

Others may largely work from home or base themselves away from the university in London, for example, for proximity to decision-makers, splitting their time between a campus in the regions and central London. Some public affairs colleagues are largely external-facing which may mean they are less engaged in the internal processes and rhythms of the university which frees up time and energy. Consultancies can also make a big difference to your work, though they come at a price. Think carefully about whether some budget for targeted activity which fits with your objectives could add value, amplify, or give your work some extra muscle. The flip side of the restructuring and refocusing of resources in the sector currently is that it can open up opportunities to make the case for the impact your work is having and seek more resource through internships or even apprentices – a great way to help your university spend its levy and engage proactively in the Government's skills agenda.

Beware of burnout

Be clear about your objectives and how much you can realistically achieve. You simply cannot do everything and risk burning out if you try to. Entering into a newly created function can be overwhelming, as there is so much you could do and there will be excitement and unrealistic expectations from your colleagues about what can be achieved and how quickly. This is an area I am still working on but discussing long-term objectives and priority areas of work with both executive and line-manager colleagues is surely part of the picture to ensure there is a shared understanding of what is important and how much can be achieved. Having the confidence to say no to areas of work that don't fit with these priorities is important and, where possible, delegating and sharing work with other teams such as internal communications, community, and corporate engagement. Own your professional expertise and judgement with confidence and set clear parameters about what can and can't be done and where your limited resource is best spent.

When you work alone with limited resources in a new role, it is doubly important to stay motivated, happy, and healthy to ensure you can maximise your impact with the resources you have. Reflecting on your learning and development can support this. Most universities have training, mentoring, and other activities you can get involved in and there are sector-wide initiatives through Advance HE, for example, which are worth a look. It's fair to say ours is a niche profession and next steps in terms of professional development are far from obvious. I remember my shock at once meeting someone else who worked in public affairs for a university at a friend's party. Getting involved in peer networks such as the Lighthouse Policy Group or other public affairs networks can help you reflect on your own development and next steps within this very particular profession, as well as supporting your work and providing ideas to try out in your own setting. It can also create opportunities to establish yourself in your own right in the sector through speaking at workshops, getting involved in organising national conferences, blogging, or writing on your role or the issues you are working on.

Depending on where you sit within the university, it can also be challenging to build a social network in the workplace and especially when you are less likely to be part of a broader team of people working in the same field. If you sit with the senior team it may alienate you from other colleagues at times. In the same way that it is crucial to share your work, I have felt more supported since I started making more of an effort to get to know my colleagues on a personal level. With today's challenging external environment, colleagues in universities often share the same hopes, fears, and frustrations about the sector, and talking about these together can help keep things in perspective.

Conclusion

Two years into my role I have helped the university to influence policy on apprenticeships, Brexit and immigration, transnational education, London's skills challenges, and T-levels. The university has hosted visits from the Universities Minister, Department for Education, Ministry of Justice, local MPs, and the chair of the education select committee. It has also made history, creating a global media storm while giving oral evidence to Parliament with a robot witness, alongside its students, executive dean, and industry partner. It has also hosted the launch of the university's strategy in London's City Hall with high-profile speakers and stakeholders in attendance. Middlesex has submitted 11 consultation responses and counting, and written evidence to four parliamentary inquiries. The public affairs function is understood by the leadership team, senior managers, and colleagues working in communications and marketing, corporate engagement, and on apprenticeships. The university is more consistently and effectively engaged in key representative membership bodies at both national and regional levels.

But there is much more to do! Planning for the year ahead is focused on amplifying our public affairs work through the media and developing proactive thought leadership on key issues that the university cares about. There is work to do around our relationship with key employers and capitalising more on our expertise in transnational education. In terms of my personal development, I am fighting a daily battle to make space to move out of operational mode and think strategically. I am also keen to improve my work–life balance and learn to switch off more easily when my head is fizzing at the end of a busy day. It can be overwhelming getting a new function off the ground in a modern university but the reward comes when the slow and steady drip-drip of building relationships, networks, and messaging pays off and you get traction and engagement for a part of the sector and its students who rarely get the limelight and are all too frequently undervalued.

Acknowledgements

With thanks to the following colleagues for their reflections and expertise in policy and public affairs which have informed this chapter: Liz Shutt, Director of Policy, University of Lincoln and Greater Lincolnshire Local Enterprise Partnership; Dr Caroline Carpenter, Director Policy and Information, Solent University; Louise Cordell, Corporate Communications Manager, Solent University; Jonathan Woodhead, Policy Adviser, Birkbeck University of London; Angela Martyn, Associate Director, External Relations and Stakeholder Engagement, Middlesex University London.

CHAPTER 13

The influence of universities in a civic context

Selena Bolingbroke and Tess Winther

Introduction

The concept of the "civic university" is not a new phenomenon. There have been a number of different drivers of the civic university, from the late-nineteenth-century and early-twentieth-century "red brick" universities prioritising technical and engineering skills in large metropolitan locations (Birmingham, Bristol, Liverpool, Leeds etc.), to the wave of new "plate glass" institutions (East Anglia, Essex, Kent, Warwick, York etc.) alongside the establishment of polytechnics in the 1960s which provided for expansion of higher education (HE). While the twentieth-century notion of the civic university focused on equipping students with the skills to serve local industries, the twenty-first-century civic university extends its reach and opens up both the community to the university and the university to the community. This is an essential development because, as a sector, we cannot afford to neglect the wider narrative around the value of universities that goes beyond the production of graduates.

The last 20 years have seen a succession of policies and funding-led interventions within the HE sector to support the civic agenda – the Higher Education Business and Community Interaction Survey, Higher Education Active Community Funding 2002–06, University Challenge 2008, and, more recently, the Higher Education Funding Council for England (Hefce) collaborated with the Local Government Association (LGA) to support the Leading Places programme. While these policies led to a greater focus on local impact and activity among universities, arguably they have reinforced a view of this as "third-leg" activity – discretionary, and of implied lesser value than the first two core legs: teaching and research. We contend that universities must demonstrate their value to the public and evolve their narrative of knowledge production and knowledge sharing to meet the challenges of their local communities now and in the future; it is vital to the discourse around maintaining public trust in public institutions – universities can be on the front line here, with the potential scale and reach to influence public views in a way few other public-purpose institutions can.

The Goldsmiths story

In this chapter, we will relate the story of Goldsmiths University of London's development of a community engagement strategy and consider its impact. Using Goldsmiths as a case study, we also consider why the civically engaged university is of value to itself, the HE sector, and the public. Goldsmiths is a small university of around 10,000 students based in New Cross, South East London, with a focus on arts, humanities, and social science. The "Goldsmiths Institute" was established in 1891 by the Worshipful Company of Goldsmiths and its objective was "the promotion of the individual skill, general knowledge, health and well being of young men and women belonging to the industrial, working and poorer classes". Also worthy of note was the commitment to allow "artisans, handicraftsmen and apprentices" to be admitted at half fees. Richard Hoggart, Warden (equivalent of vice-chancellor) of Goldsmiths College from 1976 to 1984, was a seminal figure and his background in adult education and the establishment of Cultural Studies as a discipline made him a "uniquely qualified" figure to lead Goldsmiths (Firth 1991, 129).

The impact that Hoggart had on the culture of the institution lived long beyond his tenure as Warden: this was the culture where the contribution and relationship between Goldsmiths and its local community was valued. Moreover, the notion of civic values was entwined with the cultural identity of the Goldsmiths' mindset. However, over time and driven by changes in national policy during the 1990s, Goldsmiths strove to be recognised as a research-intensive institution with the new predecessors of the Research Excellence Framework dictating prestige and funding, and internal policy and behaviour became increasingly dissociated from the institution's historically civic roots. The identification of being research-intensive, coupled with the growth in student numbers, both domestic and international, detracted from the values of civic engagement. While Goldsmiths was successful in cementing research excellence and growth in student numbers, Patrick Loughrey, Warden from 2010 to 2019, recognised a need to revive the university's original mission and roots in the local community. Loughrey talks about the "indelible emotional DNA" of public institutions being tied to their founding principles, a concept he was introduced to in his previous role as Director of Nations and Regions at the BBC.

For Goldsmiths, the revival of the civic mission meant reprioritising the importance of engagement between the university and the local community so that the impact of the university's transformative and radical education would be felt locally, as well as nationally and internationally. There was also the recognition of a changing relationship between the public and universities felt more broadly in society. The increase in undergraduate tuition fees from 2012 created the impression of the cash-bloated university sector, paying its "fat cat" vice-chancellors at the expense of students' mounting debts. Post-Brexit referendum analysis identified the level of education as one of the key points of distinction in the characteristics of Remainers and Leavers across the country, with graduates much more likely to vote in favour of Britain's membership of the EU, showing the division between those who inclined to create their identity "anywhere" compared to those who were only equipped to identify with "somewhere" (Goodhart 2017).

In 2014, the recognition of the need for a refocus on the civic materialised as a new Community Engagement strategy and, in 2018, following consultation with staff and students, Civic Engagement was elevated to a key strategic theme in the new institutional strategic plan. This positioned civic engagement as a means of enhancing the university's endeavours to improve the student experience or the pursuit of research excellence rather than detracting from the prestige or quality of the institution. It encouraged Goldsmiths and all its members – students and staff across academic and professional service departments – to explore new ways of creating touch points with the local community and for the institution to create "more doors" into the campus community. These doors came in the form of physical facilities open to the public – a new cinema, art gallery, theatre – but also included better access to existing resources – a community membership scheme for the library, a web portal to support matching students who wanted to volunteer with local community and voluntary sector organisations that had opportunities to use their talent.

Goldsmiths recognised that to be *of* our community, rather than just *in* our community, the need was to exert positive influence and consider how the totality of institutional activity affects the community. Embedding civic responsibilities across the institution drew on activists and champions from academic and professional service departments, and utilised our long-established research centres which have expertise in community engagement and urban renewal and development. Although there were small funding streams available internally for individuals to bid for to support small community engagement projects – our Annual Fund supported by Goldsmiths alumni and donors and administered by Goldsmiths students' union – the steer from the strategy was for the university's departments to think about how their mainstream day-to-day activity could be delivered differently. For example, the procurement department redesigned its supply-chain approach to address the needs of small local businesses; the History department established a series of local walking tours as a key part of their undergraduate teaching. There was also a steer to create more spaces for internal dialogue and collaboration – a new Community Engagement Forum was established to aid this, as well as a forum for Public Engagement in Research.

To celebrate achievement, Goldsmiths created Public Engagement Awards and the students' union now recognises community volunteering in its annual student award ceremony. Internal communication is a challenge – despite being a small university it can be difficult to keep track of activity happening across the institution; the internal forums were established to support information exchange and bring together the internal advocates and activists to share their experience. Although staff and students had been engaged in projects and activities which benefited the local community over many years, the activity lacked profile, coordination, and the continuity of a collective approach. The strategy provided rationale and articulation of the mission and a collective purpose that channelled the power and influence of these activities.

Partnerships

> Working with Goldsmiths has been a pleasure and I do think the partnership has moved to a higher level in recent times. At a dinner with some fellow Local Authority Leaders and London Higher it became clear to me that our relationship was qualitatively better than in other parts of London and that is only possible because there is a willingness to work together on both sides.
>
> Sir Steve Bullock, Mayor of Lewisham 2002–18

Strategic external partnerships within the community were essential to the implementation of the strategy. These partnerships allowed Goldsmiths to reconnect with the issues that mattered to the community; the university was able to contribute to existing civic activities as well as co-create new initiatives. The first strategic partnership was with the London Borough of Lewisham. In 2015 the Executive Mayor and Goldsmiths' Warden agreed a memorandum of understanding to underpin the relationship and commit to areas of collaboration. Goldsmiths is a valued partner of the Council and contributes to all the major partnership boards across the borough – from the Safer Lewisham partnership to the voluntary and community sector Stronger Communities Partnership, and most recently the Lewisham Poverty Commission. The memorandum gives practical expression to the warm words and high regard that were felt but previously not consistently acted upon.

From this foundation, Goldsmiths and Lewisham Council went on successfully to apply for the LGA and Hefce-sponsored Leading Places programme in 2016–17. This enabled a focused response to the issue of local economic inclusion which was a key recommendation of the Lewisham Poverty Commission.

Results of this work include: an initiative to leverage joint procurement power to benefit local small businesses through hosting targeted "meet the buyers" events, providing specialist creative entrepreneurship expertise to local small businesses through the Lewisham Council Enterprise network, and workforce commitments around apprenticeships and payment of the London Living Wage. The relationship between Lewisham Council and Goldsmiths is no longer restricted to a "skills and education" agenda. The university is a key partner in terms of delivering the council's ambitions around placemaking, job creation, and economic development. The partnership has faced challenges and withstood changes in senior personnel – changing Mayors, Chief Executives, and Wardens – but has a thriving group of staff who are "opposite numbers" in both institutions and who work closely together and meet regularly to review the progress made on shared objectives.

A new forum arose from the Leading Places programme – Lewisham Leaders, established to bring together all of the "anchor" organisations in Lewisham. As a result, better working relationships between Goldsmiths and other anchor institutions, such as the local hospital, college, and two large housing associations, have been forged. Partnership has been the means of starting and, more importantly, sustaining a conversation between those anchor institutions, all of which are focused on local public benefit, about what the biggest local demands and challenges are and how together they can work collaboratively to find solutions and have the most impact. The next stage for Goldsmiths is to extend this strategic partnership work into the relationships it has in the voluntary and community sector.

Student and staff engagement

> It's a pleasure working with Goldsmiths and an exciting proposition ahead to better connect students and staff with local needs and aspirations and put skills and experience to good use for local benefit.
>
> Sam Hawksley, Lewisham Local

When consulted, the surrounding community always cites access to students as their number one priority. Goldsmiths students volunteer thousands of hours to projects and groups in the local community and the university is a key partner in Lewisham Local, a forum established to connect the community through the spirit of giving and by volunteering their time and skills. One student society – Hacksmiths – has hosted community hackathons addressing challenges such as social isolation identified by local community organisations and also runs a weekly coding club which is open to students and members of the local community. The Student Ambassadors Scheme and the widening participation and outreach team facilitate tutoring opportunities at local schools, campus visits, student shadowing, and mentoring. These are paid positions allowing students to engage and develop during their degree on a flexible basis. Goldsmiths recognises that the majority of students are not able to volunteer their time on a regular basis, or for free, and that this does not diminish the act of engagement. Outreach to local schools and colleges has always been a strength at Goldsmiths and every year over 3,000 local pupils engage with some form of Goldsmiths activity whether on campus or in their classrooms. Other examples include: a regular Saturday art club for young people; community gardening; sponsoring kit for a local young football team; and creating bespoke music production projects for young people at risk of exclusion from school.

To support local sustainability, Goldsmiths staff give talks to local schools and businesses on sustainability issues and a regular collection drive for our local food bank is organised. The community values the expertise, talent, and energy of Goldsmiths students and staff and vice versa. Student placements included Pepys Community Forum in Deptford, mapping LGBTQ safe spaces in Lewisham, and work with the London Youth Support Trust in Peckham to support local young entrepreneurs. Civic engagement at Goldsmiths is naturally reciprocal because everyone learns from the interactions and projects by valuing the input and experience brought by others. Goldsmiths students are increasingly aware of the value civic engagement adds to their university experience alongside their academic activities; the university has seen an increase in community-based activities being presented as part of students' Higher Education Achievement Record (HEAR) portfolios.

Shared space

> It is great to have a large, multi-skilled organisation supporting local initiatives. It increases the local group's feeling of self-worth and opens avenues of work and activities that might not otherwise be possible.
>
> Clare Cowen, Brockley Society

It is notoriously hard to quantify the impact of community engagement, but evaluation of qualitative data proved insightful when refreshing the Goldsmiths strategy. Consultation with local community groups that had worked with Goldsmiths over the life of the first community engagement strategy – not a comprehensive list, but a range of interests from the Lewisham Education and Arts Network, the Telegraph Hill Festival, Pepys Community Forum, New Cross Ward Assembly, Lewisham Local, and the Brockley Society – made it clear that there were high expectations of the role that we could and should play in the community and that physical access to campus and facilities is highly valued by the community.

Goldsmiths operates a community discount scheme for room bookings in addition to hosting events and meetings for local groups and organisations from school sports days to local food network conferences. In the academic year 2017–18, the value of such lettings was in excess of £50,000. Local residents can access the university library and archives through a community membership scheme, and a recent relaunch and local promotion saw a threefold increase in membership, demonstrating local interest and appetite. The consultation also enabled residents to voice frustrations on certain issues such as living on a street with a non-stop-partying student house or living opposite a part of the campus under construction. Goldsmiths wants to maintain positive relations and the consultation enabled a response which became the "good neighbour" policy. The estates department changed its way of working and now ensures that future construction disruption is minimised by more sensitively scheduled deliveries and traffic management. Sharing space has allowed for new connections between local community groups and the Goldsmiths staff and student communities to be made and allows collective development of a strong voice on local issues such as the threatened closure of our local hospital and the threat of gentrification to local estates.

Open and shared learning, teaching, and research

> It was interesting to see how the young people on the "What's the Story?" project very quickly went from wanting to be met at the front of the building to taking ownership of the public spaces both in the campus grounds and the Stuart Hall building. I'd be interested in exploring some soft handover "through the gate" activities where academics work with community group in their space and then there is a follow up activity on campus.
>
> Sarah Lang, New Cross Ward Assembly

A perennial challenge of external and civic engagement in a community with a perpetually changing makeup is to let people know what Goldsmiths can offer them. A consistent platform was launched through the new community listings magazine aimed at local residents to promote and welcome them to the wide range of public events, lectures, and exhibitions. Much of the output is performance-based and Goldsmiths students and staff need and want to perform for full-house audiences, so the university put a lot of effort into getting more of our local community along to events. Small initiatives led by academic staff have been wide and varied, from creative writing workshops with Millwall Football Club fans, to canal-side community walks, or local citizen engagement with research on air-quality monitoring, to holding a "People's University" engaging people in the university's latest research, including local sound-system culture and Lewisham people's history and everyday heroes at the annual Lewisham People's Day festival. In and of themselves, these might be seen as small standalone projects, but some will develop into more substantive permanent offers. For example, Goldsmiths Open Book works with people at the margins of society, often from offending or addiction backgrounds. Its model of self-empowerment is about helping people realise their own strengths rather than imposing ways of being upon them and its ethos is "education for education's sake". Open Book has grown over the years from being a largely externally funded project based at Goldsmiths, arguably with more recognition outside the university than within it, to becoming an established Goldsmiths department with a tailored foundation year enabling access to the Goldsmiths Integrated Degree programme for learners without formal entry qualifications.

Goldsmiths recognises its responsibility as an advocate of learning and knowledge within the surrounding community and that collaboration will develop skills and ideas, and integrate the university into its surroundings, co-creating new communities. Through engagement with local festivals and local libraries, new links have been forged to support our Public Engagement in Research programme. It is important to us to share, exchange, and promote knowledge and skills, to enable local people to access our programmes and our public lecture series, as well as our world-class research. One particular example of the latter stands out: the commemoration in 2017 of the fortieth anniversary of the Battle of Lewisham,[1] an event of real significance in the local community. Goldsmiths organised a range of activities to initiate dialogues with the public about how the battle should be remembered. Dr John Price and the Public Engagement in Research team organised a series of events leading up to and across the anniversary weekend, which culminated in the unveiling of a permanent Lewisham Council commemorative plaque on Clifton Rise attended by over 300 people. A citizen journalist project "What's the Story?" was created involving Lewisham Libraries, Goldsmiths School of Journalism, and the local ward assembly which engaged local young people in creating media around the commemorations and materials that have been integrated into the curriculum used in local secondary schools. As a whole, the project brought together 15 local organisations, including Lewisham Council and the Albany Theatre in Deptford, as well as dozens of individual musicians, artists, educators, and researchers. Total attendance was well into four figures, with many audience members providing valuable feedback and contributing their memories and ephemera relating to the anti-racist movement of the late 1970s. One attendee of the weekend said: "I think it is wonderful that Goldsmiths have worked so hard to bring the anniversary events to such a wide audience, especially in these times of such uncertainty again." The commemoration led to new local collaborations and the discovery of new film footage taken on the day.

Conclusion

We have shared some examples of how our current and developing think-ing has worked in practice. We encourage universities to define their civic identity and duties, being mindful that, in our experience, this act of defi-nition should be co-created with the stakeholders of both the internal and external communities in order to resonate fully. Our community is a tab-leau of smaller diverse groups and we need to acknowledge the positive and negative disruption we cause in our communities. We gain from our ties to place, and defining our civic mission is as important as other "third-leg" activities such as knowledge exchange and industry engagement. For Goldsmiths, the civic identity of the university started long before the strat-egy. However, the strategy offered a common platform from which we could communicate and listen as an institution. We believe that universities are microcosms within their communities with the power to coordinate and facilitate initiatives and collaborations. Universities may be the homes or creators of the "anywheres", but they belong to their localities too; place is part of identity and the "civic university" mission locates identity within a community.

There is a danger that universities develop borders that separate them from their surroundings. Civic engagement is not only activity but an ongo-ing dialogue and exchange of ideas and initiatives. Symbiotic priorities and collaboration will create synergy between partners, communities, and insti-tutions. Civic engagement is much more than benevolent community engage-ment projects. A strategic approach and visible leadership are imperative, but these must be combined with grassroots champions across the institution. The value we have seen in a "whole institution" approach, as opposed to locat-ing ownership for community engagement activity in a single department, is that it creates a more sustainable strategy, with recognition of organisational self-interest as well as community benefit. For Goldsmiths it has led to greater external engagement links and awareness across faculties, the student body, and professional service departments. Ties will manifest and ambassadors for the institution will emerge. They will tell of their experiences gained and of the new ideas yet to be fulfilled, creating a virtuous cycle. Universities need to be more conscious of their power and influence and tactical as to their deployment and impact.

Note

1 On 13 August 1977, the far-right National Front (NF) attempted to march from New Cross to Lewisham town centre, leading to violent clashes with counter demonstrators and the police. The Battle of Lewisham, as it became

known, marked the first time an NF march was prevented from reaching its destination, and also saw the first deployment of riot shields by police in England.

References

Firth, AE (1991) *Goldsmiths' College: A Centenary Account*. London: Athlone Press.

Goodhart, D (2017) *The Road to Somewhere – The Populist Revolt and the Future of Politics*. London: Hurst & Company.

CHAPTER 14

Influencing policy is core business for universities

Ant Bagshaw

Introduction

Across the chapters of this book, the case has been made in different ways that there is a need for universities to engage with policymakers and the processes of policymaking. In England especially, the Higher Education and Research Act 2017 and its associated regulatory regime – the creation of the Office for Students (OfS) in particular – have changed the terms of universities' relationship with the state. No longer is there a "buffer body" in the form of the Higher Education Funding Council for England (Hefce), said to have been "captured" by providers (Morris 2017); universities now have a regulator with many sticks, but few carrots. Hefce was not universally loved, however, particularly by smaller providers which were known to complain of its inflexibility of approach. It also had effective mechanisms for concentrating research funding which reinforced the status quo of the university hierarchy in England, again something which some providers benefitted from and others resented. The growth in the university-based "policy wonk" preceded the creation of OfS, but it is in the context of the new regulatory regime that investing in work to influence the external environment is no longer an "optional extra" but a core function of the university, one which should be given appropriate prominence and resource in the context of strategy formulation and implementation.

One way to look at the higher education (HE) sector in England is to see the shift in regulatory attention from institutions to students. In the past, the state funded universities (through various mechanisms of grants as well as via students' loans), and these funded students' teaching, associated services, and academics' research. Now, students are the focus: money follows the students in the form of tuition fee loan vouchers; students use the information available to them to make choices in the marketplace; some providers will succeed and others will fail; failure, known euphemistically as "market exit", is considered a sign that the system is working. The marketised HE system: so far, so simple. But from the point of view of universities, this demotion – or neglect – in the regulatory context is not a comfortable position. They have existed and wish to continue to exist (rather than opting to fail), and they also have a mandate – either by virtue of their charitable objects or, in a small number of cases, shareholder interest – to fight for their survival in whatever conditions are given by the regulatory environment. While the regulator may have little interest in institutional survival, universities have a clear imperative to pursue their own success.

While this is most starkly present in the English context, I argue that it is a necessary competence for all universities to have a policy-influencing and public affairs function. As large businesses (a term which is not universally welcomed in HE) – even the smallest institution with a turnover in the millions, to a few in the billions annually – with thousands of staff to pay, students to teach, research to pursue, and communities to enrich, there is a reasonable case that there should be a corporate view of what the external environment should look like to advantage the university. Having taken a view, there should be associated activity to: 1, try to make those conditions come about; 2, try to minimise the damage of any negative consequences.

There are limits to the areas which a university might consider its external environment. First, those limits will be topic areas: there are policy questions such as the immigration regime for international students, or research funding policy which are *directly* linked to institutional success as they impact on the financial and reputational health of the institution. Beyond the very direct policy concerns, there are topics, some of which may be peripheral to university interests, which affect institutions but less directly. These may be the provision of cultural or sporting facilities in a city, or the quality of secondary education regionally. Universities should not necessarily engage on *all* of these matters, or indeed pursue each with equal vigour; external engagement and policy influencing should be seen as both for a corporate benefit, and as part of the broader mix of civic activities. The second constraining factor is the spatial dimension: it may be that a university should focus its efforts on the immediate locality and the economic opportunities and public services in the environs of a campus. On a national level, as well as the HE sector's regulatory conditions, a university may have a legitimate interest in engaging with environmental policy or international relations as they relate to the conduct of research and education. The exact locus of influence will vary by the particular situation of the university and its priorities, but an interrogation of the areas where influence would be valuable is an important early step in developing the strategic approach.

This chapter – read in the context of the book and the tools, skills, and perspectives described in the other chapters – aims to present some ways of thinking about how to shape the *institutional* view and, more importantly, what it means to develop the capacity for influence at the most senior levels within the university.

Strategy

It is not acceptable – as a strategic position on the part of a university – to keep one's fingers crossed and hope for the best. Rather than wait for conditions to change, be they regulatory conditions, funding, market forces, or political fads, it is incumbent on universities to try and influence their external environments. The essential reason for this is that the conditions may get worse, rather than better, if universities sit back and refuse – or neglect – to engage with the external policy environment. It is also worth noting that in some cases the game may be "zero sum", meaning that the institutions which have been most active receive the greater spoils either financially or in some other form of preferential treatment. The opportunity cost of non-engagement may be high; the absence of a strategic approach means that it will be impossible to understand the costs of lack of engagement. If unmoved by the existential need to develop policy influence, universities should consider the good that they can do in their communities and regions: through their activities in teaching and research, and through their convening power, universities can achieve significant positive outcomes for the population at large. Combining enthusiasm for policy influence with the civic agenda should be both good in itself – and a bulwark against further declining trust in institutions – and also a key support for the businesses of the university.

For the vast majority of institutions, the primary focus of external influencing efforts will be at a local level. The university needs to nurture positive relationships for obtaining planning permission, accessing funds, providing services to students and staff. As well as obtaining preferential services or additional resources, influence should aim – as part of a university's long-term positioning – to build its reputation as an engaged party with knowledge, insight, and capabilities which can be of use to other actors in the system. The strategy then may not take an approach of "we want X", either because there is not an immediate need or because the nature of the relationship would not sustain an ask in this manner, but "we want to be seen as Y" which, in the short, medium, or long term may be useful as a way of building alliances and establishing relationships. For larger or more complex topics, it may be necessary to build a coalition of partners and, therefore, knowing the right people in the right other organisations will be a way of supplementing the university's own direct influence. Beyond the immediate locality, some universities will also have a clear regional partner such as a metro mayor or Local Enterprise Partnership with which to engage, and this may well be next on the list of priority stakeholders. Mapping these relationships and understanding their relative importance to the university should facilitate decisions of what resources to spend on each level, when, and how.

While the "glamour" of lobbying might take place in a capital city, the desire to "do" influence should be tempered by a realism about what could be achieved, and from what reasonable investment of resources. The foci of attention vary by institutional location, history, and priorities: universities in the UK's devolved administrations, for example, will likely have a much closer relationship to their national governments, a product not just of a (broadly) more benign relationship than in England but also a result of there simply being fewer institutions, and therefore each one able to obtain proportionately greater time with the relevant minister or civil servants. This level also needs to take into account the relationship with third-party organisations such as mission groups and representative bodies (on which more later).

Having considered the levels at which a university might want, or need, to engage with its external policy environment, the greater prize for an institution's strategic approach is in the ability to consider this work from the point of view of the whole institution rather than just on the part of individuals who are charged with the work coordinating or enabling these activities. Therefore, when thinking of policy influence in the context of university strategy, it is useful to interrogate what strategy documents *do*, and what strategic thinking *does*. Rather than, say, write that "we will influence policy" within a five-year forward-looking document, it is valuable to consider the actions or behaviours which would be necessary for effective influence, and also what outcomes the university expects. As well as being of lower value – that is, a less productive use of the resources put into the activity – it is entirely possible that an unstructured view on engagement may have negative effects. A narrow focus which wastes the time of stakeholders, for example by bombarding politicians with requests or complaints, or one which promotes initiatives which are of interest to the university but not those it is trying to influence, may leave external actors with a less positive view of the institution than if nothing had been arranged.

I propose a maturity model in Table 14.1 as a way of elevating thinking about policy influence towards the outcomes that a university wishes to achieve, and what the underpinning activities will need to be.

Table 14.1 Policy influence maturity model

Maturity	Activity	Outcomes
Accidental	The university may have influence on its external policy environment, but there is no knowledge of this work, or interest in supporting it.	The university has positive and negative influences on its environment, but there is no capacity for, or interest in, tracking this impact.
Passive	The university has ambition to influence its external policy environment and some individuals do this within their sphere of influence, but it is not coordinated.	Individuals or groups within the university influence the external environment, but not explicitly to serve the corporate needs of the institution.
Active	There is a coordination of efforts to influence the external environment including explicit strategic goals which are communicated to appropriate staff. There is some tracking of activity.	The university can identify positive impacts through tracking the effects of activity against stated strategic goals.
Embedded	Staff across the university know and understand the institutional strategy, including where and how to influence outcomes for the better. Relationships are tracked and nurtured. Monitoring is undertaken with reporting at the most senior levels. Staff are recognised for their time and effort towards external policy influence.	The university, through mature and authentic relationships, is able to demonstrate a direct link between its activities and positive outcomes in key areas such as funding and regulation. There is a culture of positive influence which further sustains the activities and builds institutional knowledge and capacity.

Culture

To achieve the most mature approaches to external engagement and policy influence, universities should adopt – and promote – a culture which recognises the importance of the activity and demonstrates to colleagues that the work is valued. As with other elements of culture, that recognition needs to come "from the top" with an understanding among vice-chancellors and executive members that they may need – even when it is not an activity that they are naturally comfortable with – to devote time and energy to developing skills in this area. It continues to be possible for an outward-looking senior leader in a university to engage extensively, but without the structures in place to ensure that those activities are conducted to serve the ends of the institution, or fail to bring the insights from those activities to bear on how others do their work and plan for future influencing work. And it has been equally acceptable for leaders to say that this is simply not a priority, or that they would like to delegate the work to a sole member of staff, or to a third party. Neither model, of the enthusiastic sole trader or the neglectful introvert, should be seen as acceptable to meet the terms of a modern university.

One way to think about building up a culture of engagement is to see its place in the university as a learning organisation (Laurillard 1999). The evolution of institutional research, particularly in the US (e.g. the Association for Institutional Research), is a further way of conceiving of the university as an organisation which interrogates its activities in a rigorous way, learns, and improves. Looking outwardly, to draw ideas from other institutions – in HE, in other sectors, from around the world – should be a central part of trying to influence externally and to build a dialogic system. External influencing isn't simply about transmitting "this is what the university wants" but about developing the listening and interrogative skills so as best to situate the university's wants and needs within its external context. To start, this may involve "listening exercises" where staff approach key stakeholders and ask for feedback about how the university is operating; using a third party here is also an option to provide some distance in pursuit of honest answers. The information needs to be gathered and analysed, ideally with a willingness to hear "hard truths" about the level, quality, and frequency of engagement and what could be done to improve. This approach can be most successful when the university has developed a culture of self-interrogation so that there can be sophistication, authenticity, and consistency of message. With this culture, and the appropriate leadership, the university can build the effective platform for its influencing work.

Resources

There is of course a limit to the amount of time and other resources which the university should devote to external influencing activity; the argument that it is core business is to make the case for embedding the activity, not for letting it dominate or drive institutional behaviour. It will not normally be necessary to have a large internal team, to have expensive contracts with consultancies providing services in public affairs or public relations, or to invest in extensive marketing campaigns on policy issues. This work supports the mission of the university by aiming to achieve the best possible conditions in which research, education, and the other areas of university operations are able to flourish. However, where universities are large and complex organisations, it is reasonable to allocate a proportion of time from the executive to engage in influencing activity, and it is now normal to invest in at least one professional services post to coordinate and shape this work. In addition to internal resources, the most effective universities draw on a wide range of external resources, many of which are covered in detail elsewhere in this book: media organisations (e.g. Wonkhe, *Times Higher Education*), think-tanks (e.g. Higher Education Policy Institute), alumni, community stakeholders, politicians, and opinion formers. These can be, separately or simultaneously, sources of information and channels of influence; a sophisticated campaign will understand the politics of a policy area through engagement with well-connected third parties, and then use a range of techniques – face-to-face meetings, events, publishing opinions – to attempt to shape the debate to the university's advantage. The universities which nurture and leverage their connections are the ones better able to use them to achieve influence.

Working with mission groups is a hedging activity, one which should not be seen as the wholesale outsourcing of external influence at the national level. There will be times when the university's aims are at odds with the mission group; it may be that the group is simply uninterested, too divided in its members' views or under-resourced for the task. In these cases, the university must have its own independent approach. Similarly, the representative bodies such as Universities UK (UUK) suffer from a larger and diverse membership. Securing a consensus which satisfies all members will be difficult, if not impossible. In 2018, the fragility of UUK's approach was demonstrated when its energies became consumed by an industrial dispute over the Universities Superannuation Scheme (USS) (Kernohan and Bagshaw 2018). In this instance, UUK formally represented employers in the USS process of its revaluation and proposals for amending retiree benefit; half of the universities in UUK experienced strike action related to USS. For those universities for which the USS dispute was not a material problem, there was significant frustration about the way in which the issue – albeit recognised as a very serious one – consumed almost total attention from the organisation to the exclusion of other agendas. Influence can come through working with others, either in permanent or semi-permanent organisational structures like mission groups and representative bodies. But an over-reliance on these organisations presents risks to member universities; a strategic approach will balance these risks, ensuring that the institution is not over- or under-exposed to one channel of influence.

Conclusion

The traditional model for external policy influence by universities has been a benign amateurism where hope and accident have been primary tools for policy influence. That is no longer acceptable. Universities should accept that external policy influence is core business, both to further their own institutional success and as a tool for effective positive outcomes as part of their wider mission to do good in society. To achieve this, universities should build into their strategies and operations:

1. capacity for self-interrogation to develop as learning organisations;
2. resources, both from specialist staff and the time of senior leaders, to participate in external influencing activity;
3. aspirations to achieve an embedded approach to external influencing, one which is systematic and sustainable.

Given that the needs and skills outlined here will likely become even more important in the future, it is essential that the people leading universities engage with the question of policy influence. Future university leaders should actively develop their own skills and knowledge, as well as consciously support others' development, to ensure that they are confident and capable to succeed in this area.

References

Kernohan, D and A Bagshaw (2018, 3 March) A beginner's guide to the USS dispute. *Wonkhe*. Available from: wonkhe.com/blogs/a-beginners-guide-to-the-uss-dispute/

Laurillard, D (1999) A conversational framework for individual learning applied to the 'Learning Organisation' and the 'Learning Society'. *Systems Research and Behavioural Science*, 16, 113–122.

Morris, D (2017, 2 April) Deliverology in, out and around the university. *Wonkhe*. Available from: wonkhe.com/blogs/deliverology-in-out-and-around-the-university/

Index

Page numbers that reference tables are in **bold**; Page numbers that reference figures are in *italics*.

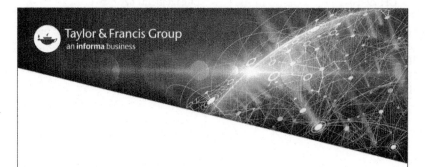